To Dominic Kelly
with best wishes from
Roy Cossar
France to England
1980 13 42 41 m

We own Laurentic

by Jack Scoltock

in collaboration with Ray Cossum

ISBN 0 948154 52 7

Printed and Published by
Impact Printing
Coleraine & Ballycastle

Front end paper: The *Laurentic* under construction at Harland & Wolff, Belfast.

(Photograph supplied by ©National Museums and Galleries of Northern Ireland, Ulster Folk & Transport Museum, negative ref. no.H1343)

Back end paper: The *Laurentic*.

(Photograph supplied by ©National Museums and Galleries of Northern Ireland, Ulster Folk & Transport Museum, negative ref. no.H1350)

FOREWORD

Mention the name LAURENTIC and ears prick up in maritime history circles and diving fraternities. So many stories and myths have been told and written about this particular ship that she has acquired almost legendary status. The truth is that what was initially a huge marine disaster involving tremendous loss of life and human suffering eventually became a benchmark for courage, tenacity, skill and daring in man's battle with the elements. The reason was easy to explain - the ship was carrying a fortune in the form of over 3200 bars of gold when she was sunk!

'Yard number 394' went down the slipway at Harland and Wolff's Belfast yard on 10th September 1908. The ship was originally laid down as the ALBERTA for Dominion Lines but passed to the ownership of the Oceanic Steam Navigation Co., better known as White Star Line, and completed as LAURENTIC. This magnificent 14,892 ton ship was powered by triple expansion steam engines and her three screws could drive her through the water at a very respectable 17 knots. She was 565 feet long with a beam of 67 feet and could accommodate 1660 passengers in three classes. She was the latest of this company's majestic vessels, built specifically to serve their North Atlantic routes and few who were on board when she was handed over to her owners on 15th April 1909 could have imagined what fate had in store.

LAURENTIC offered luxury, comfort and reliability to the many thousands who travelled across the Atlantic on board her. Apart from the wealthy and the famous who crossed on her, one noteworthy passenger was Inspector Dew of Scotland Yard, who boarded the ship at Liverpool in July 1910 in his bid to reach Canada ahead of a slower ship known to have on board suspected murderer Doctor Hawley Crippen. The speed of LAURENTIC and the novel use of the new Marconi wireless telegraph system were to keep the nation captivated for over a week with the details of the chase to arrest Crippen. This story makes fascinating reading here also.

Fast enough to outrun any submarine, LAURENTIC was selected by the Admiralty in 1914 to fulfil the role of transport and later as auxiliary cruiser. In the first role she transported German prisoners and nationals from West Africa and later fulfilled the duties of an auxiliary cruiser in the Indian Ocean and Far East prior to returning to home waters where she was selected to carry a large consignment of gold bullion from Liverpool to Halifax, Nova Scotia.

Shortly after sailing from the Royal Navy's base in Lough Swilly in County Donegal on 25th January 1917, after a stop-over, the LAURENTIC struck a mine laid off Fanad Head by U-80 and sank within an hour taking with her 354 men and 43 tons of gold.

The story of the ship, the sinking and the various dangerous and exciting salvage attempts to recover the gold, extending over eight decades, is wonderfully recounted within these pages by diver Jack Scoltock in collaboration with Ray Cossum, who had devoted years to diving and researching the wreck.

At the time of writing interest in the wreck has seldom been greater with the recent re-discovery of the ship's safe at a depth of over 40 metres. This will be recovered soon and there are those who think that it may contain the remaining 25 bars of gold missing from the previous salvage attempts.

The story continues to fascinate all with an interest in shipwrecks and salvage whilst the headstones and memorials in churchyards and cemeteries around the Swilly stand as silent but potent reminders of the original incident which shocked the communities there during the dark days of the First World War.

Robert Anderson

Portstewart

Contents

Also available

Shipwrecks of the Ulster Coast
by Ian Wilson

Donegal Shipwrecks
by Ian Wilson

Impact Printing
Diamond Arcade
Coleraine BT52 1DE
(028) 7034 4543

CHAPTER ONE

ORDERED TO HER DOOM

In 1989 a letter from the Guinness Book of Records, addressed to RAY COSSUM, stated that the 1990 entry in the *great* Book would read as follows:- 'The record recovery in terms of gold ingots was that from the White Star Liner, H.M.S. *Laurentic,* which was mined in 40.2m/132 feet of water off Fanad Head, County Donegal, in Ireland, 1917. Since 1917, 43 tonnes of gold (3191 of the 3211 ingots), have been recovered by the Royal Navy, COSSUM Diving Syndicate and Consortium Recovery Ltd.' This information was partially incorrect as neither Cossum Syndicate nor Consortium Recovery Ltd. had recovered any gold. However, the name, COSSUM was to be synonymous with *Laurentic.*

On 22nd March, 1969, at his home in, Dunmore Gardens, Derry, Ray Cossum received a telegram from his brother Eric which would set them on a quest for gold that would last for over thirty years. The words were: WE OWN *LAURENTIC*=ERIC.

The Cossum brothers had searched for over three years for the White Star Liner, *Laurentic* and the tragedy of the 14,892-ton liner is well recorded. It was laid down in 1907 as The Dominion Lines *Alberta* and was then transferred to

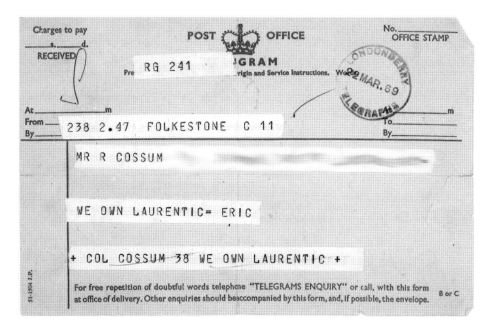

White Star in 1908. She was completed by Harland and Wolff as the White Star Lines, *Laurentic,* and had her maiden voyage on 29th April, 1909, from Liverpool to Quebec and Montreal. The great cruise liner was 550 feet long (169m) and 67 feet (21m) in beam. It had three propellers, and two four-cylinder triple expansion engines exhausting steam into a low pressure turbine that was to become a standard feature in many of the White Star's Liners. The *Laurentic* was fast enough to outrun any submarine, one of the reasons it was later converted to an armed naval ship.

An early example of its speed was shown to the world in 1910, when *Laurentic* was involved in the capture of the famous 20th century murderer, Doctor Hawley Crippen. It was also the first murder case in which the Marconi Telegraph was used.

Dr. Crippen was an American and, with his wife Cora, moved to 39, Hilldrop Crescent, Holloway, London, in 1905. Mrs. Crippen, a particularly robust lady, who was known to be unfaithful and particularly mean to her quiet husband, ran a guest house. Within a year Doctor Crippen was seeking comfort from his secretary Ethel Le Verve. Their love affair carried on for almost five years before Crippen began events to do away with his wife. On 17th January, 1910, he ordered several grains of a poison from a New Oxford Street chemist. When he collected the poison two days later, he signed the chemist's register. Two weeks later Crippen pawned some of his wife's jewellery for £3,500. On the 2nd. February, Crippen's mistress turned up at a Music-Hall Guild, where Cora was a member, with two letters not in Mrs. Crippen's handwriting, telling the Guild that she had had to go back to America because an aunt of hers was ill and that she would have to resign from the Guild. However, as the weeks went by, Cora's Music-Hall friends began to grow suspicious, more so when Crippen attended a ball that was run by the Guild. Crippen's partner at the ball was Ethel, and shortly after she moved into Hilldrop Crescent, and they began to call themselves Mr. and Mrs. Crippen. A month later the "Crippens" went on a week's holiday to France and on the day they left a friend of Cora's received a telegram telling her that Cora had died in America and had been cremated. But Cora's friends grew more suspicious until one of them eventually contacted a friend of hers at Scotland Yard, and asked him to investigate the "Crippens". His name was Inspector Walter Dew. He duly visited Crippen at Hilldrop Crescent, where Crippen told him that Cora had left him for another man and he had made up the account of her death to avoid stories of scandal. Dew believed him, but a week later he decided to pay Crippen another visit. When he got there he found the house empty and later, when he went to Crippen's place of work, he was amazed to find that Crippen had instructed his partner to wind up their business because he was going on a long journey and would be away for some time. Dew later found out, through questioning staff, that Crippen had asked one of the office boys to purchase clothing suitable for a large boy. Highly suspicious, the Inspector returned to Hilldrop Crescent and, during a search of the house, found a pile of flesh and hair under bricks in the cellar. But there were no sign of the bones. When the hair and flesh were examined it was found that the body was that of a female who had had a stomach operation. Traces of Hyoscine, a powerful poison, were found in various organs. After the examination Dew immediately ordered a warrant for Crippen and his mistress. But it was too late. Crippen and Ethel Le Neve had disappeared and Dew suspected they had left the country.

On 20th July the S.S. *Montrose* set sail from Antwerp to Quebec. The ship's captain, who was called Henry George Kendall, made it his business to speak to all the first class passengers. An amateur detective, he noticed that two of his passengers, Mr. Robinson and his son John, were behaving improperly and walked on the deck hand in hand. From the bridge he noticed that Mr. Robinson occasionally squeezed his son's hand. He also noticed that Mr. Robinson had recently shaved off his mustache and was not wearing his glasses. Judging by the marks on his nose he had worn them until recently, and so Kendall became suspicious that the Robinsons were not what they seemed. The case of the murder of Crippen's wife had been well reported but where the doctor and his mistress had gone was a mystery. Unable to keep quiet about his suspicions, Kendall had a wireless sent to Scotland Yard. The wireless read: *Have strong suspicions that Crippen London Cellar murderer and his accomplice are among saloon passengers. Accomplice dressed as a boy, voice manner and build undoubtedly a girl.*

On the 23rd of July Inspector Dew boarded the *Laurentic* at Liverpool and the fast liner gave chase. The journey took 8 days and every day of the exciting chase was reported in the newspapers.

As the *Montrose* streamed into Quebec, the *Laurentic,* with Dew on board dressed as a ship's pilot, overtook her. Captain Kendall knew from an earlier search of the "Robinson's" cabin that Crippen had a gun, so the reason for Inspector Dew's disguise was his plan. Earlier Kendall had invited "Robinson" to come and see the pilots arrive on board. When they did Kendall invited the pilots to his cabin and then sent for "Robinson" to meet them. Kendall described to reporters what happened. "When Crippen entered the cabin I said, 'Let me introduce you.' Crippen reached out his hand and Dew grabbed it. The Police Inspector removed his pilot's cap and said, 'Good morning, Mr. Crippen. I am Inspector Dew from Scotland Yard. You know me.' Crippen was shocked but then he said, 'Thank God it's all over. I couldn't stand it any longer.'"

The *Montreal Star* later reported that when Crippen was being led away from the *Montrose* he spat out a curse to Captain Kendall. "You shall pay for this treachery, sir!"

Crippen's trial opened on Tuesday 18th of October, 1910. His only defence was that there was no proof that the body in the cellar was his wife, but after a trial which lasted four days, the jury found him guilty. His mistress, Ethel Le Neve went free after a one-day trial on 25th October. Crippen was hanged in Pentonville Prison on 23rd. November, 1910, by John Ellis.

Four years later, the Liner *Empress*, with Captain Kendall at the wheel, was passing the same area where Crippen had been captured, when a bank of fog suddenly enveloped the huge ship. The time was 2.14am. Within two minutes it had crashed into a Norwegian coal boat called the *Storstad*. As the two vessels broke apart, Kendall tried to beach the *Empress,* but 15 minutes later the *Empress* rolled over and sank beneath the St. Lawrence, taking over 1,000 people - the majority of whom were fast asleep at the time - to their deaths. Later several newspapers posed the question: Did Crippen's curse cause the ship to sink?

Thirty years later Henry Kendall wrote his memoirs. The title was, 'I caught Crippen.' He lived until he was 91 and died in 1965 in a London nursing home.

At the beginning of the First World War the British fleet moved from Loch Ewe to Lough Swilly and it was off the coast of Donegal that several great sea battles were fought. It was just off Bloody Foreland, Donegal, that the first British Dreadnought battleship *Audacious,* one of only two to be lost during the First World War was mined. The date was October 27th, 1914. Sinking, she radioed for help.

It was dark, cold and with a high swell it was almost impossible to evacuate the men. But as dawn broke an enormous Liner accompanied by four destroyers appeared and it was late morning before that White Star Liner, *Olympic,* with the help of one of the destroyers, managed to get a 6-inch line to the stricken vessel. It was attached with over ten of the biggest shackles and strongest cables available and within an hour the *Olympic* began to try and tow the *Audacious* to safety. But the wind that day was gusting and the swell had increased. Progress was painfully slow. All the time, as the battleship sank deeper into the water, the men were being evacuated until all but Captain Dampier, the chief officers and around forty seamen, remained. Suddenly towards dusk the *Audacious* swung around and the wire snapped. Rafts were quickly built in case the *Audacious* sank during the night and a decision was made that the rest of the men on board would be taken off and some would be returned in the morning to try and secure hawsers to three tugs that were on their way from Belfast. But the tugs failed to arrive in time and at 8.30pm that evening there was a sudden explosion, and the 22,000-ton battleship keeled over and sank in less than thirty minutes. When it was later proven that it had been a mine that had caused the initial damage to the *Audacious,* there was an urgent response from the Admiralty. They were shocked that one of their greatest Dreadnoughts could be so badly damaged by a mine that orders were signed to build up the number of their mine sweeping vessels and by 1916 over 700 minesweepers were on duty.

A month after the *Audacious* sank the *Laurentic* was taken over, on November 16, by the Admiralty, and from December, 1914, until January, 1915, she was used for transporting German merchant seamen and prisoners from the west Coast of Africa to England. Her patrolling duties began in February, 1915, until August, 1916, sailing around Hong Kong and Singapore. Part of her job was to stop any suspicious merchant ships and remove enemy aliens. From August she was used for transporting gold bullion from South Africa and England to Halifax, Nova Scotia, with the exception of a short patrol around the Caribbean in October, 1916. Two months later, on the 4th of December, her Commander John Mathias, aged 49, was killed in a fire on board. No-one could get word to shore to inform his family because, during the fire, the radio had been damaged. When the ship docked the officer-in-charge told a shocked Mrs. Mathias of her husband's death. With her was her eleven-year-old daughter, Anne Marie.

The Saloon of the *Laurentic*.

(Photograph supplied by ©National Museums and Galleries of Northern Ireland, Ulster Folk & Transport Museum, negative ref. no.H1353)

The last voyage of the *Laurentic* was to make her more famous but for a very different reason. She was to carry 3,211 gold ingots from Liverpool to Halifax, Nova Scotia, to pay for munitions that Britain urgently needed in their efforts to defeat the Kaiser. The value of the gold bullion was £5,000,000.

The final voyage of this huge liner lay around the northern fringe of Ireland, where three of Ulsters counties - Antrim, Donegal and Londonderry - meet at the sea. It was a lonely stretch patrolled by German U-boats waiting for any unsuspecting craft to enter their area. The main submarine command lurked off Malin Head, the most northerly tip of Ireland, and the way into the calm protected Lake of Shadows, Lough Swilly. Across the mouth of the Swilly three trawlers supported a boom of heavy nets through which no U-boats could penetrate, and it was for Lough Swilly, and the village of Buncrana, that the *Laurentic* headed. The reason for stopping off in the Lough is explained here in a letter written by Augustus F. Dent before he died. Augustus was a survivor of the doomed ship and later worked as a diver during the salvage operations.

"Just after we left Liverpool we received a wireless from Admiralty to call into Lough Swilly to discharge four ratings who had left Chatham Barracks. Their names were, Seaman G. Ford, Seaman Maidement, Seaman G. Pike and Seaman C Lomerton. They had contacted (spotted fever) so we diverted our course to Lough Swilly. On arrival we landed the ratings whose O.F. numbers were included in the signal. The S.M.O. ashore told us to weigh anchor and proceed further to Buncrana as there was a submarine outside the Lough (waiting for us)."

As the great ship eased towards Buncrana all those on board heaved a sigh of relief. Captain Reginald Norton looked at the calendar in his cabin which showed, Thursday, January 25th, 1917. Safely moored in the Swilly many of the officers took boats into Buncrana and headed for the Lough Swilly Hotel to have a pleasant meal and a drink or two.

Water inspector, Mr. Hugh Doherty, then a ten-year-old messenger boy, remembered the *Laurentic* moored in the Swilly. "She was only here a couple of hours when she was ordered out without an escort - straight to her doom."

One of the maids who served the officers in the Swilly Hotel was Mrs. Tom Jones, nee Rebecca Longwell, who later went to live in Aberdovey, Wales. She said, "The officers were having a meal and were in good spirits when the message came through that the *Laurentic* was to sail that night. The officers didn't expect it and it was a shock. They all left quickly and they certainly didn't seem too happy about it."

As Buncrana people were sitting down to tea the *Laurentic* got ready to sail. Soon it was heading past Dunree Point, through the safety boom, round Fanad

Head and out towards the wild Atlantic Ocean. Captain Norton gave orders for full speed ahead not knowing that a submarine. built at the Vulcan Wharf in Hamburg 1914, under the command of Hedrich Von Glassnapp, had left Germany 12 days before with 28 mines, and on the 24th of January, had laid out the last 6 in mine-field 45, which lay just outside the entrance to Lough Swilly. Glassnapp had left immediately for his base at Heliogoland after the last mines were in place.

Augustus Dent remembered that night. "It was bitterly cold, a rolling black frost. We were to proceed on orders from the S.M.O. to pick up an escort (a destroyer) outside the Lough. At 5pm a signal came from the S.M.O. to proceed. When we got to the entrance, going 16 knots, we could see Fanad Lighthouse. Suddenly a Tin Fish (torpedo) hit us midship. The ship went over about 20 degrees. All the lights went out and engines stopped. What a crash! It was impossible to lower all lifeboats. Then we were hit again (Tin Fish in the port side). The ship even keeled then thank God and we were able to lower all the lifeboats. This was around 6pm and it was very dark. A snow storm was blasting at us with a wind force 12. Orders were shouted to abandon ship. My mate and I and another Petty Officer called G. Riddlesworth, found the after starboard boat full up hanging from the davits so we took charge and lowered the boat halfway then shinnied down into it. Then we waited our time to release the dropping gear. We were very lucky to drop on an even keel. What a job we had to keep her from going under the stern. When we eventually rowed clear we saw a light astern away to our port quarter so we pulled for it." As his men scrambled onto the lifeboats, Captain Norton hurried below to free the prisoners and to check that all his crew were on deck. The Captain, true to tradition, was the last to leave.

Dent again: "We pulled for the light, rowing for all we were worth and making good headway. A few minutes later we heard an explosion of the boilers or perhaps it was the magazines as the ship sank. Suddenly someone shouted, *Breakers ahead!* so we sheared off and that made us all downhearted. It was freezing cold and we rowed until we were exhausted. My hands were bleeding with the strain of trying to row against the strong wind and I didn't realise until later that one of my toes had been crushed. But we all knew that if we fell asleep we would never wake, up so we kept alive by singing "Nellie Dean" and other old favourites. Between songs, flares were sent up, but as the last one petered out there was no sign of rescue."

Out in the open sea many of the men shivered to death. Augustus was lucky to have survived, but 354 of his shipmates either froze to death, were killed in the explosion, or were drowned. Back in Buncrana Dr. James McCormick, at the naval base, had just finished his dinner when he heard the principal medical officer shouting, "Get down here quickly!" Dr. McCormick, who had watched the *Laurentic* sail up the Swilly earlier said, "There was a long wait but as the survivors came in we gave them hot drinks and tended to their injuries. The unfortunate dead were taken to the basement of the Lough Swilly Hotel and I had the job of searching them to identify who they were. Altogether I registered 71 deaths, however, there were three we couldn't identify. It was really the cold that killed them. I cannot remember a colder spell. It must have been 12 degrees below freezing. But I'll never forget the next afternoon when, around 2 o'clock, a trawler came in with a lifeboat in tow. There were 24 bodies on board. Only two of the men were alive." That trawler was called *The Morning Star*, and taking part in the search Mr. Paddy Murphy, who lived at West End Terrace, Buncrana, recalled, "The deck was a terrible sight. Bodies were piled high. We had a boat in tow and the sailors were sitting in position frozen at the oars." Later Paddy, who worked for the Navy, was to help pull the cart carrying some of the salvaged gold ingots from Buncrana pier to the Naval Yard for dispatch to Belfast.

A cabin on the *Laurentic*.

(Photograph supplied by ©National Museums and Galleries of Northern Ireland, Ulster Folk & Transport Museum, negative ref. no.H1353)

The funeral was the largest ever seen in Buncrana. It started at eleven o'clock from the pier where the survivors and victims were first landed. The procession was headed by a detachment of troops with arms reversed and, as they slowly marched along, a military band played the Dead March in "Saul". Behind the band came two motor ambulances containing the bodies of three officers, enclosed in oak coffins, and enveloped in Union Jacks. Then followed twelve Army Service Corps wagons conveying the bodies of the various naval ratings. The bodies were all covered with the Union Jack and numerous wreaths. Immediately after the remains walked the 120 survivors, officers and men, with the exception of the Captain, who had gone to England. The men were dressed in the clothing which had been provided for them by the mayor and citizens of Londonderry. Following them came the mayor and mayoress of Londonderry, a county court judge, the admiral in charge of the district, the officers of the naval and military staffs, representatives of local and district public bodies, coastguards and police.

Large crowds of people lined the route and, as the cortege passed, they reverently uncovered their heads in honour of the brave departed. When the band had finished playing the solemn music of the Dead March, pipers commenced a Highland lament.

Grave of *Laurentic* crew at Fahan, Co. Donegal

Some schoolchildren were excused lessons to watch the procession wind slowly along the four-mile road to Fahan graveyard, where 68 of the 354 dead were buried. One man who remembered the scene was Mr. Andy McGlinchey, who lived in Upper Main Street, Buncrana. He recalled the procession passing Ballymacarry school. "When we heard the band the teacher said we could all go out and watch. I was about six years old then but I'll never forget it. The band was in front and behind came two Red Cross ambulances, then 12 gun carriages drawn by horses. Most of the coffins on the carriages were draped with flags. Behind them came most of the survivors walking four abreast."

At Fahan graveyard, beside the site of St. Mura's Church dating back to early Celtic Christianity, the coffins were buried in a huge pit. Two Church of Ireland ministers read the offices and two Presbyterian ministers read Scripture. Two Catholic priests recited prayers, gave Absolution and sprinkled holy water on the coffins. When the service was over the military band played, "When our heads are bowed with woe" and the troops joined in the singing. The firing party then discharged a volley and afterwards the band played the first verse of, "Peace, Perfect Peace." Then came another volley and the band played again. After a third volley another band played the third verse of this hymn. The firing party then fixed bayonets and presented arms, as the Last Post was sounded.

The funeral was a sad affair but it brought relief for one man who believed his son was being buried with the others. He went over to thank the mayor for all he had done for his boy and told him that he had come from Dublin too late to identify the body. His son, who was very much alive, saw him with the mayor and ran to greet him. Apparently the names Callaghan and O'Callaghan had been mixed up and, in the confusion, the rating's father had been misinformed. At the funeral were three Irish women who had walked all day and throughout the night to get to Fahan to claim their dead. They were dressed in the fashion of remote country districts, wearing large woolen shawls. They stayed at the graveside long after the public had gone, praying over the graves of their sons. Many beautiful tributes were sent by the surviving officers and men, the naval and military officers of the district, the troops of the district and a number of leading people of the district. One wreath bore the inscription, "In loving memory of our fallen shipmates from four who are left to carry on." This wreath is reputedly to be from the four ratings who had been put off at Buncrana. Another wreath read, "To the undying memory of the officers and men of the *Laurentic* who perished January 25th."

For months after, the sea continued to give up its dead. The beaches around Lough Swilly were littered with bodies. These were usually buried in the country graveyards. One body, that of Lieutenant William A. McNeill, R.N.R., was buried on a tiny uninhabited island called The Monach/Heisker Island off the west coast of Scotland.

It should be noted that when the mayor of Londonderry first heard on the telephone of the disaster and that 90 of the *Laurentic's* survivors were in a camp and appealing for warm clothing, he quickly set up an emergency comforts scheme which worked with amazing speed. Summoning the Corporation officials by telephone, the mayor requisitioned motors and the party made a round of clothing establishments and second-hand clothes shops. The mayor, himself in the hosiery business, made up a large consignment, and a hosiery firm gave a hundred pairs of socks. Soon quantities of coats, trousers and overcoats were collected. A hundred

Front centre: Mayor, Alderman A.R. Anderson, Chairman; Mayoress, Mrs. Anderson, Vice President
From left: J. McClatchie Eng., Hon. Treasurer; Mrs. D. Hevenam, Hon. Secretary; Mrs. G. Magee, Hon.
Secretary; Mrs. D. Asbourne, Hon. Secretary; Mrs. Dickson, Hon. Secretary; Capt. J. McLaughlin R.A.M.C.,
Consulting Surgeon

hot-water bottles were sent to a couple of bakeries where water was being boiled for them and a number of citizens supplied thermos flasks filled with coffee. In a short time a procession of motors was speeding to the camp. Here are the mayor's own words, told to a reporter with the *Derry Journal* of what he saw. "I found myself in the presence of what I can only call the unconquerable spirit of the British Navy. There before me was a crowd of men who had come through a terrible ordeal in which, unhappily, the bulk of their shipmates had gone down. Were they downhearted? Not a man of them. Their feelings were fittingly illustrated by a lad of 17 who, on going into the camp recreation room, walked right to the pianoforte and played, 'Pack up your troubles in your old kit bag and smile, smile, smile.' A group gathered round and joined in the chorus."

The reporter in the *Journal* reported that, "at an annual social of the local branch of the Commercial Travellers' Association the night before, at which I presided, nearly £50 was collected for the survivors in a few minutes - and there will be plenty more."

After his first run to the camp, the mayor returned with a party and took a second lot of clothing. He was gratified to learn that more survivors had arrived, having landed at remote parts of the coast. The captain and other officers were

Officers and men at the Guildhall, Derry. Each man received 1s. and a packet of cigarettes. *Journal*, 1917.

quartered in a hotel and on Saturday evening enjoyed private hospitality. By then the bodies of a large number of victims had been brought to land.

Later the mayor held a dinner for the 113 survivors, including 9 officers, at the Guildhall in Londonderry. The men were brought from the railway station by motor cars to the Guildhall and were waited on at dinner by local ladies. At the mayor's table were seated Naval and military officers including Lieutenant Walker R.N., senior officer among the survivors. After dinner the toast of, "The King" was given by the mayor and received with musical honours.

Addressing the survivors, the mayor extended to them cordial and hearty greetings not only on his behalf but on behalf of the citizens. "We are glad indeed," he said, "that so many of our brave men have been spared on this occasion and we are proud to know that in your recent trials and difficulties, which were very severe, you maintained the best tradition of the Royal Navy. That heroic spirit, that absolute indifference to danger and even death, which had ever characterised our navy since the days of Nelson, we have seen in you and all you have done. We have heard talk of a decadent race, we have been told that as a nation we were on the downgrade. All who have seen you will bear testimony that the race or nation that can produce such men as you, men of your character and spirit, will never know defeat and prove to our enemies that we are more than a match for them. I have been at many meetings in this place since I became mayor and have entertained many distinguished people, but I tell you officers and men of the *Laurentic,* never have I considered it a greater pleasure, a greater privilege and honour, than to have you as my guests today. Notwithstanding all that has happened in this unfortunate disaster, you are not downhearted or discouraged, and I hope that the same courageous, determined spirit you have shown on this occasion will possess the nation as a whole in this crisis in our history. If there is the same spirit of loyalty, devotion and self-sacrifice that you have shown, though the reward may be longer in coming than we hope for, it will come nonetheless in the form of a glorious triumph for our arms and those of our allies over those who would sweep away the great principles of freedom, justice and civilisation." The mayor went on to say that the men who were gone, including one Derry man, Andrew Steele aged 24, a son of Mr. and Mrs. Andrew Steele of 29, Ivy Terrace, had died the deaths of heroes, the noblest of all deaths, fighting for their King and country and concluding expressed gratitude to, and admiration of, the officers and men and handed to the senior officer present a bundle of 10 shilling Treasury notes, one note to be given to each man as pocket money. His worship further stated that of the 40 officers aboard only 12 survived and for these he handed over to Lieutenant Walker pocket books and silver cigarette cases.

Lieutenant Walker, replying on behalf of the officers and men, expressed his deep appreciation of the universal kindness that had been shown to the surviving members of the ship's company since they were picked up. "People have vied with each other in doing all that they could for us. While we will look back at the loss of so many fine shipmates we will have pleasant memories of the people we have been amongst and of their handsome gifts." At this the survivors stood up and cheered.

The next day two of the Catholic victims of the *Laurentic* disaster were interred with military and naval honours, practically overlooking the spot where the ill-fated vessel met her doom. One of the bodies, that of an officer, was conveyed on a gun carriage, and the other on a motor ambulance. Hundreds of soldiers and sailors, civilians, staff officers, members of the R.I.C. and local authorities, joined in the impressive proceedings. At the graveside the usual ceremonies were conducted by the military.

In their first announcement of the sinking of the *Laurentic*, officials were not sure what had happened. Here is Captain Norton's full report at the Court Martial to inquire into the cause of the loss of His Majesty's Ship *Laurentic*. It was held in the Lough Swilly Hotel four days after the tragedy.

"Sir, I have the honour to submit the following report of circumstances attending the loss at my command, H.M.S. *Laurentic.*

I arrived at Lough Swilly before daylight on Thursday, January 25th, anchoring two miles inside the boom about 7.45am. At 2pm I exercised Action Stations, darkened ship and closed all water-tight doors except those on 7 deck in the port alleyway, which have to be left open for communications. The doors between the engine room and stokehold and stokehold no.3 hold (which was full of coal) were closed. All the boats were fully equipped and each had twelve red lights, lantern, compass, biscuits, water and corned beef. The hands had been exercised at their stations on leaving Liverpool the previous day and boats turned out. At 5pm it being dusk I got under way and proceeded out of the harbour at fourteen knots increasing to full speed, seventeen and a half knots on passing Dunree Head, where three trawlers passed us inward bound. I was showing no lights of any kind, nor did I make any signal thinking it was possible there might be a submarine sheltering from a south eastly gale. I decided to zig-zag, altering first to a point to starboard and about 6 minutes afterwards 3 points to port, which made the course north magnetic. After steaming for about 5 minutes on this course at 5.55pm there was a violent explosion the port side abreast the fore mast which threw me off my feet. This was followed about 20 seconds later by a second explosion abreast the engine room the port side which caused all the lights to go out. I immediately put the telegraph to "Stop" and then, as the ship listed 7 or 8 degrees to port, "Full Astern". I then gave the order to turn out the boats and switched on the alarm gongs. I tried to call up the engine room by telephone but could get no reply from the wireless room. So telling the Yeoman of Signals, J. Burke, to fire the rocket, which he did, I proceeded along the boat deck to the wireless room in order, if possible, to send out an "S.O.S." call. There I found ordinary telegraphist W. Williams, who told me the batteries were upset and he was unable to send out a call. Returning to the bridge I told the Yeoman to call up Fanad Point Signal Station on the flashing lamp which he did, though he could not get a reply. Meanwhile some of the port (lee) boats had been swung out and lowered into the water not properly manned and I hailed through the megaphone to remain alongside but they appeared unable to do so and drifted leewards. Knowing there were 4 men in the cells under the forecastle and fearing, though the sentry had the key and orders to release them, he might not have done so, I went down there and found the men still confined. With no sign of the sentry I returned to the bridge and told Lieutenant Walker, navigating officer, to try to get a carpenter. This he did and accompanied by Mr. Porter, Chief Steward, who lighted Shipwright Harrington down to the carpenter's store where he got his axe. We broke down the doors and took the men up to the starboard boats. By this time the ship had righted itself again and it was possible to turn out the starboard boats which were ably done by Commander Rodgers R.N., assisted by Lieutenants McNeil, Morgan, James, Walker, Engineer Lieutenants Carlisle, Neil, Stewart and the remaining men. I had previously sent

Sub-Lieutenant the Hon.DeBlacquiere, lit by Mr. Porter who had a torch, to try to find out the state of affairs in the engine room, but they returned telling me the engine room was full of water and they could see no one. As the ship was getting low in the water I told Commander Rodgers to send away the starboard boats for Fanad Light and to lower the remaining one, no. 5 to abreast D.deck and wait for me. Accompanied by Mr. Porter and his torch, I proceeded below to see the state of affairs and if anyone was left. Descending the main staircase we found only a little water in the main saloon but the water was flowing along the port alleyway on D.deck from the engine room. We succeeded in closing two of the W.T. doors and then, seeing no signs of anyone, we returned and went round C.deck aft. But finding no one, and having been assured that all men had got up from the stokehold by Engineer Lieutenant Carlisle, who had been on watch at the time, we returned to no. 5 boat. Thinking the ship was about to sink Commander Rodgers had lowered into the water being the weather side and as she was in danger of being swamped I sent Lieutenant Walker and Mr. Porter into her by the life line following them myself. I was very reluctant to leave the ship like this but do not think she could have floated much longer as, by this time, she was getting low in the water. I have since heard that she has been located 4' NW of Fanad Point, about a third of a mile from where we left her. All the boats pulled in towards Fanad Point light but we were unable to weather it and there was nothing but breakers to leeward so we had to back out and were carried out by the wind and tide to the westward. Eventually we made a sea anchor with the mast and sail and rode by that. We kept the water down till midnight when it rapidly gained on us. Fortunately about this time, by burning our red lights, we attracted the attention of the steam trawler, *Imperial Queen* and Skipper A. Royal R.N.R., who came over after picking up no.16 boat, in charge of the boatswain Mr. Newing, picked us up about 1am. We cruised about to the westward till six o'clock, when seeing no signs of any boats, and being anxious to communicate with the S.N.O. and land the 62 men picked up, I directed him to proceed into harbour - there were then eight other vessels out searching. Immediately on landing I contacted the S.M.O., Captain Finnis R.N.R., telling him the direction in which I thought the boats were drifting and he gave further directions to the trawlers. All men picked up received unbounded kindness from the Officers and crew of the trawlers who gave all their clothes and I should particularly wish to mention the names of Skipper A. Royal of the *Imperial Queen*, Lieutenant J. Whitefield R.N.R. of the *Lord Lister*, Lieutenant Bibly of the *Corientes*, Lieutenant Lambert R.N.R. of the *Alpha* and Skipper Booth R.N.R. of the *Ferriby,* who behaved splendidly. Finally, I should like to bring to the notice of their Lordships the following Officers and men. Commander Rodgers R.N. was of invaluable assistance in turning out the starboard boats and afterwards in my boat, getting out the sea anchor, pulling the oar etc. Lieutenant Walker, the navigating officer, whose assistance all through to me was invaluable. Mr. Porter, Chief Steward, who was splendid all the time and whose torch was of great help. Yeoman of Signals Burke, who remained quietly on the bridge trying to signal till I ordered him into a boat. Mr. Ridgers, Chief Gunner, who rode out the night with a sea anchor. Mr. Newing, the Boatswain, who got his boat in safely and has been invaluable since, identifying the bodies. Lieutenant McNeil, the Executive Officer, who took charge of the last boat but one that left with Lieutenant James, who was O.O.W. at the time, and who thereby missed his own boat. Shipwright Herrington I have already mentioned. Assistant Paymaster Beaumont took the ship's ledger away with him in boat no. 7. It was in an airtight cylinder painted red. After he died of exposure during the night it was washed out of the boat but should eventually be recovered. He was a most excellent officer in every way. And finally Ord. Telegraphist, W. William, who is only just eighteen who, after trying ineffectually to send out an S.O.S. call, collected the confidential wireless books and brought them to me on the bridge in their iron box asking what should be done with them, waiting there some time till I told him to throw them overboard and get into a boat as at that time most of the boats were lowered. I think his conduct highly creditable and I am glad to say he was saved. Since landing we have all received great kindness from everyone. Captain Finnis, Captain Dawes, Col. Beales, commanding the camp where the men were received. The Mayor of Derry, who provided the men with clothes, cigarettes etc. Miss Craig the manageress of this hotel and her staff who have been extremely obliging and kind.

I have the honour to be, Sir,
Your obedient servant, (Sgd) Reginald A. Norton Acting Captain R.N.
The Secretary, The Admiralty, Whitehall.

Later, during the inquest, the Captain was asked was his ship torpedoed or did it hit mines. Norton's reply was, "Whether torpedo or mine I am not going to say."

However the people of Buncrana, many of whom talked to the survivors, swore the ship was torpedoed.

Later the Secretary of the Admiralty issued this statement: The fact has now been established that H.M. auxiliary cruiser *Laurentic* was sunk by a mine and not by a submarine.

News of the tragedy was kept quiet for a short time, but soon rumours began to spread of the *Laurentic's* loss of life - not of her gold bullion. That was to be kept a secret. Here is an excerpt from *The Northern Whig*, dated two days after the inquiry.

THE LAURENTIC DISASTER
SOME THRILLING STORIES.
Survivors' Terrible Experience in Open Boats.
STATEMENT BY THE ADMIRALTY.
VESSEL SUNK BY A MINE.

(Press Bureau, Tuesday)

The Secretary of the Admiralty makes the following announcement:

The fact has now been established that H.M. auxiliary cruiser *Laurentic* was sunk by a mine and not a submarine.

A Press Association correspondent wires: The White Star Liner *Laurentic,* which had been taken over by the Admiralty as an auxiliary ship, left on Thursday. The weather was fine but intensely cold. Within an hour-and-a-half or thereabouts the liner struck a mine and sank in three-quarters of an hour. Of the crew of about 475, something like 125 have been saved. Many of those lost were killed by the explosion. Perfect order prevailed throughout, the crew responding to the officers' orders with precision and loyalty.

At first, it is understood, an attempt was made to beach the ship. Meanwhile the boats were got in readiness and the Marconi installation having been destroyed by the effect of the explosion rockets for help were sent up. These were seen by the lighthouse then, and in a few minutes, a number of mine-sweepers were speeding to the scene. At the last minute before the *Laurentic* went down in 23 fathoms, the lifeboats were manned, there being accommodation for all who survived the explosion.

It was now pitch dark. The lifeboats were provided with flares and so long as these lasted it was possible to locate the small boats on the waste of water, but the rescuing fleet of mine-sweepers had almost 20 miles to cover before rescuing the nearest boats. By the time they arrived on the scene some of the lifeboats had exhausted their supply of flares. The men were taken on board the trawlers as soon as they were discovered, and the systematic searching of the vicinity resulted in one boat after another being found. The men in one of the boats were seven hours in the perishing cold before being rescued. These generally are understood to be the events following the disaster but it has to be borne in mind that the survivors among the men cannot be spoken to and that the Captain and seven other officers amongst the saved naturally have made no statements for publication.

Over 100 men were taken from the boats but no sign of any others could be seen.

Everything possible was done by the fishermen who rescued the sailors to alleviate their lot and when it became evident that no further survivors could be found all speed was made for the nearest town on the coast where a large hotel was requisitioned for the accommodation of the shipwrecked crew. The village is very small and its resources limited, so telegrams were sent to the nearest city (Londonderry). There the Mayor took rapid action. All the doctors were notified and a staff of nurses requisitioned. Every hot-water bottle for sale was acquired and stores of ready-made clothing were bought. The whole was ready in a remarkably short time and what was a veritable relief operation set out on motor cars and other vehicles for the place. Arriving at the hotel, it was found that the ship-wrecked men meanwhile had done their best to make themselves comfortable. Everything possible was done by the visiting doctors and nurses for the wounded, and it was learned yesterday that all were progressing satisfactorily.

100 BODIES WASHED ASHORE.

Telegraphing yesterday, an Ulster correspondent states - Already close on 100 dead bodies have been washed ashore and from their frozen condition there is practically no hope of any of the crew who might have been able to get clear of the sinking ship on rafts or by clinging to wreckage, having survived the very inclement weather. It is now understood that some 50 of the survivors are suffering from wounds. Whether the *Laurentic* was able to send out wireless messages for help has not been ascertained but several fishing boats, attracted by the terrible noise of the explosions, hastened to the scene. By the time they arrived, however, the vessel had completely disappeared.

OFFICER CASUALTIES

The Secretary of the Admiralty states that the undermentioned officers lost their lives when H.M.S. *Laurentic* was sunk:-

Lieutenant Commander Douglas E. Saxby-Thomas, R.N.

A grave in England of one of the *Laurentic* crew.

Sub-Lieutenant the Honorable Alan B. de Blaquiere, R.N.

Lieutenants Wm. A. McNeill, R.N.R.; Thos. Steele, R.N.R.; David T. E. James, R.N.R.; George E.R. Browne, R.N.R.; and Richard Morgan, R.N.R. Engineer-Commander Chas. E. Hurst, R.N.R.

Engineer Lieutenant Commander Geo. R. Rutledge, R.N.R.

Engineer Lieutenants Edward A. R. Larmour, R.N.R.; Herbert Sewell R.N.R.; James W. Gibbins, R.N.R.; Thomas Jamieson R.N.R.; James Carlisle, R.N.R.; George H. Daymond, R.N.R.; and Robert R. Mitchell, R.N.R.

Surgeon Frank E. Rock, M.D. R.N.

Sub-Lieutenant Laurence W. Bell, R.N.R.

Engineer Sub-Lieutenants Peter Caton, R.N.R.; George L. Elliott, R.N.R.; James R. Brown, R.N.R.; and Ernest E. Midgley, R.N.R.

Assistant Paymasters Bernard C. C. Newbery, R.N.R. and Freund Beaumont, R.N.R.

Warrant Telegraphist Richard J. Thompson, R.N.R.

(ends)

The Secretary of the Admiralty later announced 12 officers and 109 men have been saved.

OFFICERS:

Captain Reginald A. Norton. R.N. , Commander Hugh H. Rogers R.N., Lieutenant Arthur Pawley R.N. R., Lieutenant John Walker R.N.R., Engineer Lieutenant Richard Meale R.N.R., Engineer Lieutenant Harold V. Stewart. R.N.R., Surgeon William P. Starforth R.N., Engineer Sub-Lieutenant Howard C. K. Harley R.N.R., Engineer Sub-Lieutenant William Heathcot

R.N.R., Engineer Sub-Lieutenant Harold B. Evans R.N.R., Chief Gunner Arthur R. Ridgers R.N., Warrant Telegrapher Arthur Bower R.N.

The grave of Captain Mathias who died in a fire on the bridge a few months before the *Laurentic* sinking.

MEN:

Adams, Jack Bilton leading seaman, Alcock Michael seaman, Ashton Ernest do., Brushett A. H. do., Burke Patrick seaman, Burnett John Ferguson A.B., Carney James seaman, Cregan Samuel Eric seaman, Dixon Geo. Private R.M.L.I., Eillis Daniel seaman, Giddy John Robert P.O., Hodder John P.O., Kavanagh Michl. seaman, Lawrence R. William Private R.M.L.I., Lee Maurice seaman, McCarthy William seaman, McLean Donald seaman, Madden John leading seaman, Miller Wm. seaman, Mation Thomas Lowdon leading seaman, Nelson Gustive seaman, O'Reilly Daniel seaman, Pitman John seaman, Pocock William John seaman, Prior William James leading seaman, Quick Francis John stoker, Robson E.C.James Private R.M.L.I., Sheehan Edward seaman, Taylor Henry James Private R.M.L.I., Taylor William Richard seaman, Wetton James stoker, White E. George Private R.M.L.I., Woolahan William seaman.

Specially entered mercantile crew: Attridge T. J. fireman, Barber J. fireman, Brett John J. trimmer, Bruton Henry steward, Butler James fireman, Carmichael J. storekeeper, Cooke A. steward, Daniels J. trimmer, Everett Samuel trimmer, Fardell W. J. fireman, Ford Christopher fireman, Griffiths J. second baker, James J.P. assistant butcher, Kelly John fireman, Laveander P. trimmer, Lewis J. trimmer, Mahoney J. trimmer, Marney Edward fireman, Martin D. trimmer, McDonald K. fireman, McInerney P. fireman, Milnes J. fireman, Moore Thomas trimmer, Newing E. boatswain, Porter C.W. chief steward, Quirke P.T. assistant steward, Robinson W.O. chief baker, Smith F.O. S.B.A., Southwell A. M.R. steward, Stafford E. trimmer, Stephenson E. greaser, Stevenson J. storekeeper, Tildsley W.J. trimmer, Walsh Timothy trimmer, Williams William, engineer storekeeper.

The following names are published as reported:

Callaghan A. C. steward, Carmichael W. fireman, Carter C. sig., Christopher A.V. R.M.L.I., Crisp J, seaman, Davies W. H. writer, Dent A. H. P.O., Doe M. W. P.O., Dunkerley Harry musician, Evans J.M. stoker P.O., Frost G.L.S., Francis W.T. A.L.S., Gardiner T. P.O., Green E. J. seaman, Green F. A.B., Gregory A. seaman, Hancock A. seaman, Hardy T. seaman, Henery W. seaman, Hewington W. shipwright, Hewitt T. H. S.B.S., Hobbs A.A. C. sig., Jones H. L.S., Jones H. seaman, Legrove G.R. bugler, Masters P. dockyard clerk, Miller W. R. ord. telegraphist, Neil F. seaman, Nilrenz H. baker, O'Brien M. F., Richards R.M.L.I., Robinson G. A.B., Rogers G. leading signalman, Ryan Pat, Saunders Taherenner E. Private, Walker J. fireman, Warren W.J. seaman, Wood W.H. officer's cook, Wrigworth P. A. P.O.

The following ratings were landed before sailing:

Avery A. seaman, Ford G. seaman, Maidement seaman, Pike G. seaman, Somerton C. seaman. It is a sad fact that CH/17809 Private Edgar George White, 2nd. Bn. Royal Marine Light Infantry was killed in action 6 months later, aged 21. His body was never recovered and identified from the battlefield, so he is commemorated on the Aras Memorial to the Missing, France.

Two days after the tragedy the *Derry Journal* which had been at the forefront with their accurate reports of the sinking of the Laurentic published this report.

KAISER'S BIRTHDAY MANIFESTO

Amsterdam, Saturday - Emperor Karl arrived at the German main headquarters yesterday to congratulate the Kaiser on his birthday. He was accompanied by the Austrian Foreign Minister who conferred with the Imperial Chancellor and the German Foreign Secretary at luncheon. Complimentary speeches were exchanged between the Kaiser and Emperor Karl. The German Emperor referring to the Allies rejection of peace negotiations said the Central Powers would win a peace in which the bonds of friendship between them cemented by blood and iron would prove firm and true in the common work of peace henceforth.

A week after the tragedy another report in the Derry Journal read:-

SIR EDWARD CARSON AND THE MENACE

In the course of a communication expressing his inability to attend a War Loan meeting at Hull today, Sir Edward Carson, First Lord of the Admiralty wrote: "We are threatened with increasing acts of barbarity on the high seas by the enemy who has substituted the practice of pirates for the law of nations. I do not delude myself, nor will I attempt to delude you as to the danger of the German submarine campaign. These ruthless and inhuman attacks upon the peaceful ships of the world have created for us and our Allies a problem as difficult as it is grave, but this at least I can say, that the problem is being grappled with day and night by the Admiralty with tireless vigour and that our hourly anxieties only spur us on to greater and increasing efforts."

It is worth considering a report in the *Irish News* later which asked a lot of interesting questions.

A splendid Belfast-built White Star liner was sunk off the Irish Coast by a German submarine or mine late on Thursday, January 25th. This information was officially circulated to the newspapers at the late hour on Sunday night - more than seventy-two hours after the event and more than forty-eight hours after the fact of the disaster was known in the Belfast newspaper offices and to thousands in this city and throughout the North of Ireland. A list of the survivors was also sent for publication very late on Sunday night, it included the names of many Irishmen. The names of the victims have not yet been published; no doubt a very large proportion of those who perished were also our countrymen. We cannot understand the motives for this extraordinary reticence on the part of the authorities. They cannot really hope to deceive the Germans, in all probability the newspapers of Berlin and Hamburg, Cologne and Munich, Vienna and Buda-Peath have already published German-made details of the sinking of the *Laurentic*. But the Admiralty people are the arbiters of the situation, they are now under the control of a wonderful statesman and strategist whose advent at the head of the affairs was to have been the signal for a perfectly revolutionary epoch of determination and efficiency. Perhaps the epoch has arrived. The public cannot realise that things are better now than when they were two months ago - indeed there is a popular impression to the contrary - but then the public have been taught all along by the great Departments of the State that true wisdom lies in considering themselves fools. Yet we believe the people of these countries are entitled to further knowledge of the circumstances attending the destruction of the great White Star liner and the loss of its crew except those whose names appeared in yesterday's papers. It was a noble and valuable ship, more valuable a thousand times was its freight of human lives. Submarines have been noted "off the Irish Coast" at frequent intervals. What precautions were taken to secure the absolute safety of the *Laurentic* and her crew until they passed beyond that dangerous Irish Coast? No doubt the question - and others - will be asked in Parliament next week. When the *Lusitania's* crew and passengers were foully murdered off the coast of Cork, people all over the world asked the "reason why" without reference to the admitted guilt of the Germans. The *Laurentic* was a ship in service of the Admiralty; the *Lusitania* was a passenger ship. Germany's sense of honour and humanity might have been trusted - by very confiding persons - to ensure the safety of the great Cunarder; though the fact that her fate had been plainly foretold in New York must not be forgotten. But there was no earthly reason why any German submarine commander should spare the *Laurentic*. The White Star liner was "fair prey" - as naval warfare is conducted now. Was she properly guarded while within the danger zone? Questions of this kind are asked of one another by members of the public. They may be repeated "in another place." Meanwhile we can only sympathise with the families and relatives of the brave men whose lives were lost in the public service. This catastrophe is one of the most painful recorded since the sinking of the *Lusitania;* it brings home to every Irish mind the grim reality of the "submarine peril" and the terrible possibilities of the weapon upon which German reliance is now placed. (ends)

Two things that did not come out at Norton's inquiry was, how could the *Laurentic* have run into a mine when that area was supposedly secured that very morning? Why did they leave without an escort? Ray Cossum has delved into the official German records and has contacted the widow of Captain Von Glassnapp. The German naval version was that no torpedo attack was reported on that fateful day because very heavy storms prevented such attacks in the sea area off Ireland. This explanation seems to stand up with the Secretary of the Admiralty's statement. There was a lot of secrecy at that time mainly to hide the fact from Germany about the loss of the gold bullion. But the main worry was lying at the bottom of the sea. The British Government needed the gold. The war with Germany was still on and 354 Navy men had already lost their lives.

On the gravestone erected at Upper Fahan Church of Ireland graveyard in 1920 the inscription to the 68 buried there reads:

The *Laurentic* memorial at Fahan, Co. Donegal.

THIS CROSS WAS ERECTED IN THE FAITH OF THE RESURRECTION AND IN HONOURED MEMORY OF THE OFFICERS AND MEN OF H.M.S. LAURENTIC. (Capt. R.A. Norton R.N.) LOST OFF THE COAST JAN. 25 1917. UNDERNEATH REST THE BODIES OF THOSE COMMEMORATED HERE. FOR THESE AND FOR THEIR COMRADES WHO THUS GAVE THEIR LIVES FOR THEIR COUNTRY THEY WHO RAISE THIS MEMORIAL GIVE THANKS TO GOD.

Please note that quite a few of the names etched on the memoriam are misspelled. ie: Fardival should be Tardivel.

A sad fact about one of the officers buried there - Engineer Sub-Lieutenant Peter Caton is that 10 days before sailing from Liverpool on the 10th of January, 1917, his eldest daughter, Alice Maud Caton died. She was 19 years old. Peter had also served on the White Star Liner, *Republic* when she was rammed in thick fog in March, 1909. Information taken from Peter's Discharge Book No. 544278 tell us that he was born in 1876, had hazel eyes, dark hair, was 5 feet 8 inches tall, and his complexion was fair. He lived at 35, Briardalc Road, Birkenhead. All reports in his Discharge Book on his character indicate he was "Very Good". He joined the *Laurentic* in April, 1909, at Liverpool, and over the following years working as a boilermaker sailed to Portland, Montreal and New York. His death is commemorated at the Birkenhead Memorial as are four other *Laurentic* dead: Alfred Ernest Godfrey, Ernest Edward Midgley, John Magner and Charles James Wallace.

Below is the grave of Richard Firman Dodd, age 34. The Dodd family in particular had an unfortunate naval history. George Charles Dodd was lost on the *Titanic* aged 45 years.

It is interesting to note that in the graveyard on the ancient site of St. Mura's Church, Fahan, opposite, a nephew of Horatio Nelson is buried near the grave of the sailors from the *Saldanha* which sank in Ballymastocker Bay on its way to fight in the Napoleonic War. The words on Horatio's gravestone read:

IN MEMORY OF HORATIO NELSON LATE SHIPMAN OF H.M.S. ENDYMION. AN AMIABLE YOUTH WHO BREATHED HIS LAST AT FAHAN HOUSE IN THE 18th YEAR OF HIS AGE. COULD FRIENDSHIP HAVE PROLONGED HIS DAYS HE HAD LIVED. (probably should have been - HAD HE LIVED) BORN BURNHAM-THORPE IN THE COUNTY OF NORFOLK. DIED NOVEMBER 17th 1811. Perhaps another story lies with young Horatio's death.

Also in Fahan Church, beside the christening font, can be seen a painting of the *Laurentic* and below it a poem called, The Loss of The Laurentic, by W.R. Latham.

The Loss of the Laurentic

In nineteen seventeen the proud
Laurentic
Was bound from Ireland to the USA
When the Germans sank her out in the
Atlantic.
Off Donegal one bitter winter day

None saw the swift torpedo that destroyed her
None saw the submarine that launched the blow
They only felt the shattering explosion
That stopped the engines throbbing heart below

The wounded vessel quivered paused, listed
Plunged to her death beneath the hungry waves
And in that fearful wilderness of water
300 gallant soldiers found their graves

A precious ship, precious lives were lost there
And lost the precious cargo in her hold
Five million pounds of gleaming glittering ingots
Three thousand, two hundred bars of gold

The finest divers in the british Navy
Skilled men of courage and tenacity
At home in that strange world of
swirling water
Were sent to wrest that treasure from
the sea

They dared the hazards of the winds, tides
Of shifting sand, strong current floating mine
Of cutting edges that could mean disaster
Of falling wreckage fouling pipe, line

For seven years they battled to recover
The wealth that lay there wasting in the deep
Until at last they freed those prisoned riches
The jealous sea had fought so hard to keep

Man by his skill can build an ocean liner
Man by his skill can send her to her doom
Can by his skill bring back the buried treasure
But not the dead from their untimely tomb.

W. R. Latham

In nineteen seventeen the proud *Laurentic*
Was bound from Ireland to the U.S.A.
When the Germans sank her out in the Atlantic
Off Donegal one bitter Winter day.
None saw the swift torpedo that destroyed her
None saw the submarine that launched the blow
They only felt the shattering explosion
That stopped the engines throbbing heart below.

The wounded vessel quivered paused and listed
Plunged to her death beneath the hungry waves
And in that fearful wilderness of water
300 gallant soldiers found their graves.

A precious ship and precious lives were lost there
And lost the precious cargo in her hold
Five million pounds of gleaming glittering ingots
Three thousand and two hundred bars of gold.

The finest divers in the British Navy
Skilled men of courage and tenacity
At home in that strange world of swirling water
Were sent to wrest that treasure from the sea.

They dared the hazards of the winds and tides then
Of shifting sand strong current floating mine
Of cutting edges that could mean disaster
Of falling wreckage fouling pipe and line.

For seven years they battled to recover
The wealth that lay there wasting in the deep
Until at last they freed those prisoned riches
The jealous sea had fought so hard to keep.

"Man by his skill can build an Ocean Liner,
Man by his skill can send her to her doom,
Man by his skill can bring back the buried treasure,
But not the dead from their untimely tomb."

    I think that final stanza of Latham's poem really makes one think about the tragedy of the *Laurentic* and the futility of war.

Here is a true story told to me by the grandson of Patrick and Margaret Henderson. In August, 1939, Paddy and Maggie and their four teenage daughters were on a short holiday in Fahan. It was mid-way through the holiday and on a beautiful summer's night the girls were sitting on a low wall enjoying the late evening sunset and watching out for any of the local lads. The sky was just turning pink when suddenly the youngest girl felt the hair crepe along the back of her neck as she looked down the road. With a choking cry she pointed and all the girls saw a group of sailors marching in formation up the road towards them. For some reason the sight of the sailors frightened them, though the girls had often seen sailors in their hometown of Derry. Screaming with fear, they ran to their lodgings. There they told their parents what they had seen. The following evening, on a visit to a friend's house, Patrick told a group of around 12 people there about his daughters seeing the sailors and being frightened. He asked what were the sailors doing in Fahan. His question had two women gasping aloud, and one trembling old man rising to his feet - his face as white as chalk. Intrigued by the their reaction Patrick inquired further. He was eventually told that the sailors were the dead from the *Laurentic* who were buried at Fahan and they only appeared as a warning when something terrible was going to happen. One man told him that the sailors had been seen a couple of years ago and shortly after two fishermen were drowned.

For the remainder of their holiday the girls were shunned by the locals.

The following month World War Two began.

Portsalon Church of Ireland Church, Co. Donegal with the *Laurentic* bell in the tower.

CHAPTER TWO

A COLD FISH

When the news of the tragedy reached the British Government they were in a panic. Britain could not afford the loss of £5,000,000 in gold bullion. It would have to be recovered and quickly. Munitions were urgently needed for, without them, the war could be lost.

There was only one man capable of retrieving the gold and top diver, Commander Guybon Damant, was that man. In 1906 Damant had set a world diving record of 210 feet during tests on the endurance of humans diving at deep depths run by the Navy. His experiences as a salvage diver were well known to the Admiralty.

Guybon Damant

Despite the danger and the fact that it was wartime, within a short period the 36-year-old Damant had gathered together a crack team of divers and crew. One of these was Augustus Dent. Damant knew Dent was a diver and had been aboard the Laurentic when she sank. He sent for him at Whale Island. Augustus recalled: "He said he wanted me to go with him because he knew I knew where the bullion room was. But the doctor would not pass me fit to dive at a depth of 30 fathoms. He said my heart was suffering from shock so that ended that. I was very sorry and went away on a Commission for two years. Later, when I joined Damant's team, I had an attack of the bends. I woke up one night with a pain and it was like someone tearing my arm off. I was carried off to the decompression chamber and kept there for about six hours. When I got out Damant handed me a glass of gin. I knocked it back and said, "Thank you sir." I'll never forget his gruff reply. "Don't thank me, it was a medical necessity, not a gratuity." He was a cold fish, was Damant."

On board the salvage vessel *The Volunteer,* Damant and his divers and crew headed towards the wreck site with orders to treat the salvage as a military exercise. Damant had estimated it would take around three months to salvage the gold, but when he arrived at the site in winter time he quickly realised his estimation was far out. Unfortunately the wreck area was exposed to the powerful force of the Atlantic tide, and strong northerly gales.

One of the first divers down was a man called, Williams. He later described the scene underwater where he found the *Laurentic* virtually intact, lying on her port bilge at a 60-degree angle. The massive blocks swinging from the lifeboats were a great danger and he found he was constantly being swept off the deck by the strong surge of the tide. However, he did manage to force a door and descend a staircase to the ship's saloon. "I stopped suddenly for, in the dim light, something had bumped against me. I began to tremble and feel colder and I almost passed out. It was a human body, and as my eyes grew accustomed to the light, I saw other bodies. It was a terrible sight. The unfortunate seamen's bodies were swollen, their eyes glaring and their hair drifting about. In fact, I nearly missed death myself, for up above in *The Volunteer* a German submarine had been spotted and the captain ordered the ship to seek shelter in Lough Swilly. Despite my presence below it was decided my life was not worth a direct torpedo hit on the salvage ship. To that end I was dragged to the surface and towed for seven miles through the water to the safety of the Swilly before being finally hauled aboard. By then I was unconscious. But two weeks later I was back diving."

It was eight days before diving commenced, mainly because of the weather.

When Damant and his crew returned to the site the weather was slightly favourable. The next diver down was called Ernest C. (Dusty) Miller. Dusty quickly found the narrow passage that led to the door of the bullion room. It was sealed

Royal Navy salvage team. Chief Shipwright "Dusty" Miller (centre) and Commander Damant (right).

Royal Naval divers with Augustus Dent (right) under the command of Com. Damant, salvage operations 1917 to 1924.

tight. On the fourteenth day of diving the door was blown out with a charge of guncotton. But now the diver found, beyond the door, a heavy latticed gate. The next day that was blown away and now Miller was able to make his way along a passageway into the bullion room. Inside he came up against stacks and stacks of the bullion boxes, each 12 inches square and nine inches deep. Each box weighed 10 stone. Though his time on the bottom was almost up, Dusty carried one of the boxes to the loading port and forced it through. Next day he managed to get three more boxes out of the strong-room in an hour. When he surfaced, and the gold was hauled on board, Damant was delighted. Now it was only a matter of sending his divers down in relays. He estimated it would take a month before all the gold was recovered. To that effect he radioed the Admiralty telling them they had reached the strong room and recovered some of the gold and it would not be long before all of it was brought up.

As salvage progressed this letter was sent to the Secretary of The Bank of Ireland.

Dear Sir,

It should be explained the ship's back is broken on its bilge so the decks are at an angle of about 60 degrees.

Submitted with reference to my telegram no. 178 dated 15th June 1917, forwarded herewith last showing numbers and weight of 209 ingots landed today from H.M.S. *Laurentic.*

The ingots will be sent under escort by rail tomorrow 16th June, 1917, for safe custody in the Bank of Ireland, Donegal Place, Belfast, Ireland.

(Sgd) Rear Admiral
From Rear Admiral, Buncrana.
To The Secretary of The Bank of Ireland.

But Damant still hadn't reckoned with the weather and the winter gales. Three weeks later *The Volunteer* had to run for shelter. The storm lasted for over a week. When Damant returned he was the first diver down. To his dismay he found the wreck had folded in on itself because of the surge of the tide and the storm. When he reached the entrance to the bullion room he found the narrow passageway Miller had walked through had collapsed and was only about 2 feet wide. When he surfaced he gathered his most experienced divers into his cabin and explained the situation. It was decided there was nothing for it but to blast their way in. It took them two weeks, but when Charlie Miller, after the last explosion, finally managed to get into the strong room he found it completely empty. Working in the darkness of the room he realised that the plating had crumpled and twisted and the gold had slid to port, down going through the decks and bulkheads until it came to rest in the port bilge. On top of the gold lay the tangled mass of first and second class decks. When he surfaced and reported to Damant what had happened the Commander was dismayed. After another meeting with his divers it was decided that the only way to reach the gold was to open a wide area through the heavy beams, working their way down until they were above the gold. As they had no cutting equipment the only way they could do this was by carefully placing small explosives within the beams and plates. The biggest problem they encountered was the heavy steel plates, many of which obstructed the diver's way down. Explosives had little effect on the plates. The only way to shift them was to lower strong lines and pull them back as far as they could so that a diver could crawl under and carefully place an explosive. This worked fairly well, although one afternoon a diver called Blachford, was cutting the

Sectional drawing showing the position in which the *Laurentic* was found lying on the bed of the sea.

Four divers who where presented with M.O.B.E. by the C in C of Plymouth due to HM the King being unwell.

wreckage away with the intention of working his way as far under a plate as he could to place an explosive when, without warning, the shackle holding the plate broke. Instantly the plate slid back trapping the unfortunate diver beneath it. When Damant realised what had happened he immediately ordered another diver to get ready. This man was called Clear. As diver Clear got ready Blachford, able to speak, called: "Give me all the air you can sir!" The pressure was increased. Then Blachford shouted: "Get another diver down here as quickly as you can!" The men listening above admired the cool way Blachford spoke. Although in danger of losing his life he had not panicked. Blachford thought that increasing the pressure of air inside his suit would cushion the great weight of the plate and save his body from being crushed. While Clear was being fitted with his diving helmet Blachford shouted for more air to be pumped down to him. But now he was being given so much air that the roar of it in his helmet was almost drowning out his voice. By then Damant was afraid the extreme pressure would burst Blachford's suit. He did not know what position Blachford was in. His suit might be pressing against a sharp piece of steel and in danger of being torn or he needed the air to keep water out of his helmet. But still Blachford called, "Give me more air!" Damant was in a quandary. If Blachford's suit was intact any additional increase of air might burst it and drown him. He decided not to take the risk so he gave Blachford as much air as he thought would not push it beyond the limits. He then turned to see Clear was ready. When the diver entered the water he carried a new line and, following Blachford's air pipe down, he soon reached him. Working as fast as he could he attached the new line to the plate. Then when he felt it was secure he called: "Take in the slack!" and moved back to watch as the wire began to slowly tighten. "Easy now!" he warned over the telephone as the plate began to slowly lift. The instant the pressure was lifted from Blachford he was hauled to the surface. Blachford had been trapped for almost ten minutes. This would probably have unnerved most divers but a few days later Blachford was diving on the wreck again.

After ten weeks the divers began to find ingots again and by the time summer was over they had managed to salvage £750,000-worth of gold.

But now, with America joining in the war, the urgency to recover the gold was not so important. Damant and his divers were ordered home and salvage for the gold was stopped until the end of the war.

Early in the spring of 1919 Damant and his crew returned to salvage the rest of the gold. This time he used a bigger vessel called, *The Racer.* Soon another £500,000 was recovered. But there was still £3,000,000 missing. The storms the following year of 1920 forced more structure down over the gold area. The storms had also deposited stone and gravel, and tons of sand, into the web-like structure reinforcing it like a concrete cover over the gold.

For a year-and-a-half Damant and his divers worked at breaking through the heavy covering. Explosives had little effect. Pumps were no good. Huge dredging buckets were used but little gold was being salvaged.

During all the salvage work Damant was obliged to send weekly reports. Below is one of these.

From....Commander G. Damant. R.F. A. *Racer,* Portsalon, Co. Donegal.

To.....The Director of Naval Equipment.

Dated....21st May 1922.

LAURENTIC OPERATIONS WEEKLY REPORT.

Submitted, the weather is rather better and we have had three full days diving this week. I have communicated with H.M.S. *Warwick* and received instructions from the Admiralty. Proceedings have been:

15th May...S.W. Gale, at Portsalon.

16th...Strong S.W. wind and squalls, unfit.

17th...Proceeded at 7.45 and worked the wreck all day clearing sand with grab, water jet and hand digging. Returned to harbour at 7.00pm.

18th...Proceeded 7.45 and moored up but after an hour's diving wind became too strong to continue.

19th...Proceeded 7.45 but found it unsafe to moor up in the heavy sea running over position of wreck. Proceeded to Buncrana, communicated with H.M.S. *Warwick*. Watered ship at Rathmullan.

20th...Proceeded 7.45 and continued operations. Returned to harbour at 5.30.

21st...Sunday. Very fine. Proceeded 7.30 and worked sand grab with divers till 4.30. Proceeded then to Buncrana. Arrived 6.30. Communicated with *Warwick*. Returned to Portsalon.

G.C.C. Damant.

Commr. (Retd)

When Damant and his crew returned in early 1922 they were pleasantly surprised to see that the area around the gold had been washed clean by sand. The heavy winter storms that had often hindered Damant and his crew had relented and helped them. Gold ingots were protruding up from the sand. That first day around twenty bars were brought to the surface. Some of the ingots were bent almost in half. By the end of the summer an incredible £1,500,000-worth had been recovered. By then the destroyer *Shamrock*, which was the guardship, had already made one run to England with a portion of the season's haul.

During that year the divers were staying at the Portsalon Hotel when one night the hotel was attacked by the I.R.A. who were apparently after the gold. The attack, however, was thwarted and they got away without any gold. But from then on the salvage team stayed on board the *Racer*, which later had machine guns mounted to its decks for protection.

Portsalon Pier, 1914.   Portsalon Hotel, 1914.

In 1923 another £2,000,000 was sent to the Treasury, leaving around 150 ingots to be found. 1924 was the last year of salvage. One of the last of Damant's reports to the Admiralty read:

From....Commander G.C.C. Damant. R.N. (Rtd) H.M.S. Salvage vessel *Racer*. Portsalon,

Co. Donegal.

To...Director of Naval Equipment Admiralty

London, S.W.1.

Date...11th, May, 1924.

SUBMITTED.

LAURENTIC SALVAGE OPERATIONS.

6TH WEEKLY REPORT.

The gold which is being recovered at the present time comes from under the wreck of the *Laurentic*. Her port side is spread flat on the sea floor and it seems that a number of bars must have passed through the port plating port-holes and accidental tears in the bilge on to the sea bottom beneath at a time when the collapse of the wreck was not quite complete. Since that time setting and creeping of the skin plating over the bottom has taken place so that most of the bars are out of reach from the holes through which they dropped and lie sandwiched between the stony bottom and unbroken parts of the ship's side.

2. We are getting at them by digging away at the sea bottom through the port-holes and cracks till space is formed for blasting charges to be forced underneath. Exploding these enlarges the apertures in the ship's side and by degrees a cavity is made between the wreck and the sea floor into which a diver can squeeze himself and clear out the loose shingle so exposing any gold there may be in the neighborhood.

A massive piece of wreckage torn away by explosives during the hunt for lost gold bars.

3. About 20 tons of stones and boulders have been raised to the surface in the course of this work and a few tons of the side plating which is so thick and tough that several blasts are generally needed to get each piece away.   G.C.C Damant. Commander.

Augustus Dent remembered his last year diving on the *Laurentic*. "Damant told me this would be the last year of salvage and that they had not seen any gold for the last month. When we got on the job he told me, "You can go down first." On the way down it was good visibility and I could see everything on the sea bed. I saw the ship's bell and also a bright object. When I got there it was a bar of gold. I said to myself, "Hallo. What are you doing there?" and the fellow on the telephone said, "Repeat." I told him, I have found a bar. He did not say anything but after a couple of minutes Damant came on and said, "Diver come up." Of course, I said, "One in the bucket, sir" and put the bar in the bucket. I came up, undressed and later, on the model, showed him where I found it. The bucket I mentioned was a one-ton bucket with holes drilled in it so it could sink. Later when I mentioned the bell to Damant he suggested we fetch it up. It was later presented to the village of Portsalon. Myself and a few of the other divers helped hang it in the tiny red tower of the church in September, 1924. I can still hear its sharp clear chimes after seven long years' of silence as it echoed around the hills."

Damant now went for the remaining gold by blasting the *Laurentic* apart until a huge area was cleared down to the sand. At the end of that year all but 25 bars had been brought to the surface. By then the Admiralty felt that it was not worth the effort or money required to keep the salvage team working as gold was worth very little in those days, and only about one percent of gold was left, so all salvage was abandoned.

This incredible feat of salvage was unequalled anywhere. Of the 3,211 ingots, Damant and his divers had recovered all but 25. Under the worst conditions possible, a

Gold bars bent by the immense pressure set up by the collapse of the sunken ships hull.

43

White Star Liner, sunk at a depth of 40 metres, had been salvaged and not one life had been lost in the five thousand dives that had taken place. Total recoveries over the seven years were 3,186 bars of gold. Recoveries were as follows:

Year	1917	Number of bars salved 542.			
"	1918	"	"	"	0 (no operations)
"	1919	"	"	"	315
"	1920	"	"	"	7
"	1921	"	"	"	43
"	1922	"	"	"	895
"	1923	"	"	"	1,255
"	1924	"	"	"	129
	Total				3,186

Number of bars that went down in the wreck 3,211.

For their troubles the ship's company received a half crown (12.5 pence) for every £100 recovered. However the divers received nothing other than a small bonus. Augustus Dent again: "I never got anything. They could have well afforded to give me that bar I found. It was the last one. All we got was our diving pay and we were also credited with one shilling (5p) per man per bar."

An article from the *Evening News* September, 1923, gives an idea of the competition amongst the divers to see who could salvage the most gold bars.

DIVER'S 200 BARS OF GOLD.

HOW "MICKIE" MADDISON WON THE CHAMPIONSHIP.

As only two dozen bars of the *Laurentic's* gold lie beneath the waves off Donegal the salvage championship between H.M.S. *Racer's* eight divers is settled.

It goes to A.B.N. "Mickie" Maddison who has recovered 200 bars of gold equal to about £500,000. His nearest rival was Petty Officer Light who brought up 170.

The *Laurentic,* which was mined in 1917, was carrying £5,000,000-worth of bullion to America, and the work of salvage has been going on ever since 1917 with varying success.

Last summer only about £600,000-worth of gold was recovered in five months, but during the past months the total recovered has amounted to something like £2,000,000.

Only a fortnight ago 400 bars were sent in boxes in a destroyer to Chatham and convoyed to the Bank of England.

A WONDERFUL DAY.

There has been keen competition between the divers throughout, but they have had to take turns according to orders, and have not been permitted to select their positions.

Very often divers have gone weeks without any success at all. Maddison owes his pre-eminence largely to a wonderful day when in two descents to the sea-bed, each lasting an hour, he secured 43 bars of gold.

Scarcely 30 years of age, Maddison has made a name for himself in Navy boxing competitions. He was employed on salvage work on the sunken German fleet in Scapa Flow before he went to Ireland. In the winter he is usually employed in training classes of divers at Portsmouth.

PRIZE MONEY

H.M.S. *Racer* is at present at Portsalon, Ballymastocker Bay, and it is understood that when she returns to Portsmouth in about a fortnight's time, her salvage career will have ended and she will be replaced by a new vessel. But the dragging over the *Laurentic* wreckage ends this month whether the few remaining bars are lifted or not. Last year *Racer's* crew received about £13 each in prize money. This year there will be a considerable larger sum.

The *Laurentic* lies 20 fathoms deep and the divers had to encounter great difficulties but the operations have been carried through without a single casualty.

(ends)

Part of the superstructure of the *Laurentic* which was blasted away by divers.

45

Another interesting article taken from the *Daily Mail* February, 1926, two years after all salvage had finished read:

HOW £5,000,000 WAS SALVED.

THE *LAURENTIC* GOLD.

FIRST FULL ACCOUNT.

DIVER HEAD DOWNWARDS IN THE SEA.

Mr. J.C.C. Davidson, Financial Secretary to the Admiralty, announced in Parliament yesterday that the cost of recovering the £4,958,000 from the White Star Liner *Laurentic,* which sank in 1917 off the west coast of Ireland while being used as an auxiliary cruiser in the war, was only £138,000 including a bonus of £6,739 to the officers and men concerned.

The work of the divers was begun in 1917. But the *Laurentic,* a vessel of 14,000 tons which had been acting as an auxiliary cruiser, was lost in a spot exposed to the full fury of the Atlantic in 20 fathoms (120 feet) of water.

STORMS STOP WORK.

For months at a time the work of the divers was stopped by storms and much of the treasure had to be literally snatched away during a lull in the gales. The work was done from the Admiralty salvage vessel *Racer,* 1,000 tons. Lieutenant Commander F.L.B. Damant R.N., himself a diver, was in charge. Commander Damant has since received the thanks of the Admiralty for his work, while several of his crew of about 50 have been decorated.

It is interesting to recall the loss of the P. and O. liner, *Egypt,* which sank off Ushant after a collision in May, 1922. She carried gold and silver valued at £1,054,000 and attempts to recover it will probaly take place this spring.

THE SALVAGE.

HOW THE *LAURENTIC* WAS SMASHED UNDER SEA.

Cmdr. Damant gave a *Daily Mail* reporter the following first full account of the salvage work:

"Diving at 120 feet is always difficult and the wreck lay two miles from land in a very exposed spot in the Atlantic. It was only possible to work for six months in the year. When we first started to work, immediately after it sank, the *Laurentic* was on its side at an angle of 60 degrees from the vertical. Using explosives we blew in a door in the middle of the ship near the strong-room. The foreman diver, Warrant Shipwright Miller, went down a tranaverse passage and eventually reached the strong-room. He unscrewed some nuts from the hinges and had the strong-room open in a few minutes. Most of the gold lay before him in boxes. It was very difficult to remove three boxes of gold. The diver had to crawl up a steeply sloping passage in pitch darkness pushing a heavy box before him and occasionally lifting it over obstacles. On the first day we removed one box and on the following three more.

Then a gale blew up from the north and lasted a week during which pieces of docking and other debris were washed on shore showing that something had happened to the *Laurentic*. When the sea subsided and it was possible to send a diver down, he found the whole ship had collapsed like a pack of cards, driving the decks out sideways. This had been caused by the enormous pressure exercised by the action of the waves deep below the surface. There was no hollow space in which men might crawl about and we had to cut a way right into the crumpled ship with explosives. Altogether and since the beginning of the operations we have removed 3,000 tons of material. In the remaining part of 1917 we recovered about £1,000,000 worth of gold.

In 1919 the work was resumed and some gold was recovered. In 1920 and 1921 we were very unlucky. When the ship collapsed the gold was divided into two sections. The first lot was comparatively easy to recover. The second consignment, however, was buried beneath about 10 feet of sand and debris, consisting of broken up fragments of the ship's fittings, including such things as berths, baths, wash-basins and tables.

"WATER IN MY HELMET".

One near-accident I remember during our salvage operations was when one day we heard a muffled voice on the telephone saying: "There's some water coming into my helmet. Only a little but be as quick as you can." We immediately sent another man down at once and he cut the pipe loose while he was standing astride it. Immediately the other man rose and the pipe dragged the second man to the surface with him. Fortunately neither of them struck the bottom of the *Racer*.

Owing to the high compression a diver could only work at the bottom about one half-hour at a time. It took him about a half-hour to come to the surface so that the pressure in his suit might be reduced by stages. During the operations we had a number of cases of high-pression sickness. These were treated by putting the affected man at once into the recompression chamber on board. He was there put under a high pressure again and very soon felt better.

Some of the bars of gold recovered were bent around into a "U" shape while others had pebbles driven hard into them and also half-crowns. One of the queerest finds was a small silver coin of the reign of Edward 11 or Edward the 1V. I do not know how it got there unless it belonged to somebody on board.

HOSE PIPE UNDER THE SEA.

The divers worked in a jagged crater in the middle of the ship, and to remove the sand they had to scoop it up in sacks with their hands. The sand was made quite hard by the action of the waves and the divers loosened it with a fire hose pipe let down from the *Racer.* The diver squirted the jet of water into the sand thereby loosening it, and as he did this, he pushed his hand into the loosened sand to feel for the gold. Sometimes, at the end of several days of work, they would have their finger-nails worn down almost to the quick, and the tips of their fingers were like soft sponges. They would not wear gloves.

In 1922, 1923 and 1924, we made good progress, and at the end of that year there was less than one percent of the gold left in the wreck. The sand was then gaining fast on the divers and the work had to be abandoned.

Throughout all the dives - and there were over 5,000 - there was not one accident, but there was one queer mishap. To prevent the pipe line from dragging on the helmets the divers tied the air pipe to a part of the wreck allowing themselves a certain amount of slack. One day a man was working head downwards when the trousers of his suit became filled with air and he started to rise to the surface upside down. When he had risen some distance he was stopped by the lashing of the pipe below and so he hung upside down half-way between the surface and the bottom like a mine."

(ends)

Commander Damant died at his home on the Isle of Wight in 1954.

In the years that followed, until 1932, the wreck of the White Star Liner remained undisturbed. In the summer of that year a retired naval officer by the name of Mallet tried to recover the remaining 25 gold bars. The Mallet company was a small one and soon the first ship he was to use was moored at Derry Quay.

Donald Gillespie, who was a young man at the time when the salvage ship *Estoy* came into Londonderry, joined the Mallet Syndicate as a deck hand. Later he became the Chief Ship's Pilot on the River Foyle. "I did it more for the romance than anything. I was a simple deckhand. They found five bars of gold. They also found a shilling which I was given as a souvenir."

Commander H. Rivers Mallet had two divers working with him. They were Mr. Tyler and Mr. Godfrey, both ex-R.N. divers, but not members of the Royal Navy team who had salvaged the *Laurentic* gold. Mr. Gillespie recalled: "The only tools the divers had was a pinch bar." (a crow bar) He remembers one incident about his work on the salvage ship. "One day the divers found the *Laurentic's* safe and, as it was about to be hauled on board, the chain suddenly snapped and it plunged to the bottom." 68 years later on the 10th of September 2000 that safe was found by divers from the City of Derry Sub-Aqua Club when employed by a television company making a film of the great ship. The safe is lying wedged amoung debris with almost three quarters of its bulk buried in the twisted steel. It is apparently unopened and will take some cutting to extract it from the wreckage. It hopefully will see the light of day in October. The find has been reported world wide and I am sure the programme about the *Laurentic* will get a bigger audience than anticipated.

The second ship the Mallet Salvage Company used was called the *Attendant*, which was not much bigger. They had no decompression chamber or an air-lift tube. However, the divers did recover five bars of gold by using the crow bars. They found the gold on the port side, where the ship's plating was lying on the sea floor. The gold was under 18 inches of shingle. These divers did not find the gold where the Royal Navy had finished their salvage, but outside the 200 yard square working area. Because the divers could not look under the side plating, they soon ran out of money. After three seasons of work and though they had found five bars of gold The Mallet Salvage Company went bankrupt.

The two divers, Tyler and Godfrey, had a pump attendant who worked the air pump while they were diving. His name was Morgan. He said that when the Mallet Company went bankrupt, their ship the *Attendant* was seized at Derry Quay. Mr. Morgan, a Welsh man, lived in Derry for several months and got a job repairing clocks as a way of making money to get back home. His son, Mr. Lloyd Morgan, who lived in Bethesda,

The *Attendant* berthed at Waterside Quay.

Bangor, Gwynedd, remembered stories his father had told him about his work with the Mallet Company and his time in Derry, and he confirmed Gillespie's account of operations, especially the lost safe.

To this present day the 20 bars lie on the bottom of the Atlantic along with *Laurentic's* safe.

CHAPTER THREE

THAT NAME HAD DRAWN US LIKE A MAGNET

Much has been talked about concerning the missing 20 bars of gold since then. An article entitled: THE GOLDEN WRECK by Harry Pugh. A PLOT TO STEAL THE GOLD, appeared in a local newspaper. In it was an interview with a man called James Dykes, from Hawkin Street, Londonderry. The article read:

WHISPER ALERTS THE THIN MAN FROM LONDON.

The tall thin man ambled casually along the waterfront, arms dangling loosely at his side, concealing the slight bulge in his right-hand pocket which hid a .38 revolver.

Through the thin fog he walked, quietly whistling. The dockyard at Londonderry was silent except for the ghostly creak of ships rising and falling on the River Foyle.

The thin man was Detective James Dykes. And as he paused to light a cigarette a figure slipped out of the darkness and whispered, "There's a plan to steal the gold. Two bars have already been snatched."

Dykes, a Sergeant in the Royal Ulster Constabulary was in charge of Londonderry detectives. He knew about the salvaging of £5,000,000 in gold from the *Laurentic*, which exploded and went down off Fanad Head in 1917.

He knew too that the salvage ship *Racer* was heavily guarded by destroyers after shots had been exchanged with three boats which came silently out of the night.

SEARCH

Sergeant Dykes, now 74, sat in his home in Hawkin Street and recalled: "I cannot tell you the name of my contact but he was a man I trusted."

"Two divers," he said, "were bribed by a dealer from the East End of London who bought them drinks and persuaded them to steal gold and pass it on to him. The gold was carefully checked when divers brought it up from the wreck to the deck of the *Racer*. After that it was too well guarded to steal. But down below there was nobody to watch the divers. Two tied cords to gold bars and fastened buoys to the other end of ropes. Then at night, when the *Racer* was at her anchorage in Lough Swilly, a fishing boat put out, found the buoys and hauled up the ingots."

Dykes wasted no time. He dashed through the fog to his headquarters and the Londonderry police swung into action.

The dealer's home was raided. Policemen searched it from top to bottom but not a trace of the gold was found.

"I believe he got rid of it before the search," says Mr. Dykes.

But he is not sure. He cannot be. For the proof lies buried in the silt 20 fathoms under the Atlantic Ocean.

Meanwhile Captain Guybon Damant and his salvage crew were in the sixth year of their long and bitter wrestle with the sea for what remained of the drowned gold.

In 1922 more than £1,000,000-worth was hunted out of the *Laurentic* debris by divers. And in 1923 they had a record year recovering - 1,255 bars each worth £1,350.

This was the year when Dykes was tipped off about the plot to steal the gold. And when Damant heard of it he was furious. He called the whole company on deck and warned that they would all lose their bonus if he found any dishonesty. Later he ordered a diver who had been seen with the London dealer to pack his bags and go.

So strict was the diving drill that not one serious accident occurred in the whole seven years of the search. Damant, though ruthless in discipline, took every care to ensure his men's safety.

The article finished on the dangers of diving to the depths the *Laurentic* divers had to go.

But, undeterred by all the information they had gathered about the *Laurentic* and its gold, Eric and Ray Cossum went to see Augustus Dent seeking first-hand information on where the main diving was done. Later, when they expressed concerns that the remaining 20 bars might have been "spirited away", Augustus told them:

"Damant was a very strict man on the divers that were working in the gold area. Only Damant and his officers knew just what was

Ray and Eric in the mid 1960s

HMS *Racer* salvage vessel.

going on down there. Divers working on the site could not move out of the gold area, which was an area of 60 feet by 40 feet unless they had a very good reason for doing so. Like the last bar of gold I found. It was not in the gold area and I had to ask Damant's permission to collect it. I would also say it was not possible to hide a bar of gold anywhere without Damant and his officers knowing that something was wrong down on the site. And when you come to think of it a bar of gold is 28 pounds weight. A diver could not throw it very far underwater. Also a diver could not walk very far without permission from up top. But another thing that would have prevented any of the gold being stolen was that there was always a Bank of England Treasury official on board the salvage boat H.M.S. *Racer* and the *Volunteer*. His job was to count each bar of gold that came up. He also took note of the part numbers so not even an officer could get away with the gold." Dent went on to say: "Some people would say a diver could have left a marker buoy to mark the spot but that would be quite impossible. Damant was no fool."

Ray says, "After leaving Augustus Dent, Eric and I were convinced the remaining bars must still be on the *Laurentic*."

Three years after they found the *Laurentic* Eric Cossum applied to the Ministry of Defence and they sold the rights of the wreck to him and Ray in 1969. The brothers formed a company called, THE COSSUM SYNDICATE LTD. Later, Ray's son, Des joined the company.

53

The day Ray and Eric found the wreck was a memorable one. Ray remembers it like this. "Standing on the stern of a small trawler heading out of Lough Swilly on the north-west tip of Ireland, gazing at the long rolling waves, my mind slipped back over the years to when my brother Eric and I were boys living in a small sea-side town on the Kent Coast with the English Channel our playground. Stories of ships and sunken treasure were more a way of life to us than to other children. How often we had joked and played at diving for gold and treasure on the 300 or more wrecks that were littered over a short stretch of coast outside Folkestone. Every conceivable type of ship lies at the bottom of the Channel, from British and German battleships to submarines and modern day liners each with their own tale of how they ended there. Back then could Eric and I have even dreamed one day our childhood games would become reality, that when we were men we would dive on a lot of those wrecks? Or that I would one summer's day in 1970 swim across the English Channel?

The trawler's engine droned steadily on as we passed Portsalon on our port side. How many times had Eric and I drank in the beautiful scenery on our way to dive over some wreck. But this was no ordinary wreck we where heading out to - years of searching and still it had eluded us - *Laurentic*. That name had drawn us like a magnet. No other name could conjure up such a fantastic story - *LAURENTIC*. The name and the mysteries that surround the great liner have become a legend of our time.

By now we where leaving Lough Swilly behind us and heading into deeper water. We could feel the high Atlantic ground swell under our feet. The search was on again. Just one more small area to cover. Would Lady Luck smile on us today? Sceptics said she would never be found again. And by now Eric and I were beginning to wonder were they right. Maybe silt had covered her? Maybe she was so flattened by the sea that she would never show up on the sounder? Even one of the greatest diving authorities in the World (who shall be nameless) had stated that the *Laurentic* would never be seen again. These questions and many more troubled our minds as we drifted slowly on out.

Ray Cossum and John Davidson with first salvage inflatable.

A good and trusted friend of mine Exporter and Shipping Agent, Tom Gallagher, whom I had been teaching to dive for the past year, had accompanied us. I had said to Tom that my brother and I were fairly certain we were onto the wreck of the *Laurentic* and would he like a "dive of a lifetime." Tom as ever was eager to come with us.

As we moved out over the site we kept our eyes fastened to the needle on the sounder. And suddenly we were shrieking with excitement as we all watched the needle climb. Could it be? Could it be HER? Quickly we inflated our rubber boat and launched her over the side. There was only one way to make sure. The Proton Magnetometer Metal Detector was rigged up. I called for our skipper, Jim Brown, to circle around the area again taking us in tow. As we were pulled behind we watched the meter anxiously. Suddenly it began to flicker indicating a massive magnetic gradient. There was no doubt in our minds now as we boarded the trawler again. This had to be it - the *Laurentic*. It had to be.

As Jim dropped a shot line Eric, Tom and I quickly kitted up. Our hearts were pounding and I could feel the half fear gnawing at the pit of my stomach as we slipped over the side. But the second I hit the water I was alright. Together we headed down into the gloom. As we descended, dull, strange shapes began to loom into view. It was her - the *Laurentic*. There was no doubt about it. I glanced at Tom. Was he using as much air as I was? I couldn't stop feeling exhilarated but I had to control it. I was breathing too hard. A quick glance at Eric told me he was OK.

Seconds later we were there. We all unashamedly hugged each other moaning like banshees into our mouthpieces with excitement and Tom and I did swimming rolls of victory. We were surprised to find we were right in the engine room. In this part of the wreck all the decks were gone. This was because the engine room was the area that Commander Damant had been working clearing all the metal decks out of the way. We also saw how Damant worked through the wreck to recover the remaining gold. He would have had to remove metal plates and then a huge amount of sea-bed shingle. This must have been a very costly salvage operation. It did make us wonder how the Mallet Salvage Syndicate Ltd. managed to find five gold bars. After all they had only an old towing tug and two divers using the old-type diving equipment. Also they used big crow bars to find the said five bars. It makes one think did they know where to look.

The wreck, when we found her, was a huge tangle of steel and metal, torn and twisted. Masses of machinery lay everywhere. One of the gigantic engines had broken loose smashing a path through the engine room to end up jammed side by side with its partner. Huge pipes and girders pointed out of the wreck and the engine room took on the appearance of a giant jig-saw. Wash-hand basins and broken porcelain from the *Laurentic's* bathrooms were strewn everywhere. Hundreds of brass shells (tons) were lying around the six inch guns, one of which was standing straight up out of the wreck like a giant finger pointing to the surface as if to warn us to go back. The other guns except that one lay on their sides.

Even today it is quite amazing how, when working in a certain area, you will suddenly stumble on a piece of machinery of enormous proportions you had never seen before. There is always a thrill of the unexpected on the great wreck. A two-ton condenser in the engine room I and other divers had passed over since our first dives was only recognized recently so busy were we with other tasks. The other two condensers weigh between 10 and 16 tons. A number of blasts have been carried out on both in order to free them from the main engine room fittings. To lift them whole is more profitable at this depth.

Only two of *Laurentic's* guns are left on the wreck now. Though they each weigh around 7 tons it is my intention to have them lifted. I intend presenting one to my own local museum in Derry and one to the Greencastle museum.

Gun at Liverpool museum

That memorable day Eric and I lifted a porthole each as physical proof of our claim of the big L.

Tom's remarks to me when we surfaced were, "Thank you, Ray. From a student diver to the teacher." It was some day and will forever stay in my memory.

Holyhead Towing Co. Ltd. with 6" gun from *Laurentic*.

The *Laurentic* then and now is like a huge football field covered in scrap. But where is the gold? Where are the 20 bars of gold and where is *Laurentic's* safe?

The quest for the *Laurentic* and its remaining gold has been an uphill task from the start. This applies not only to myself but to everyone concerned with working at her since 1917. Over a four-year period from 1973 my son Desmond has been a rod of iron in my back bone giving me the heart to continue and never ever despairing with my doubting moods. As for my wife, Bridie, words fail me - always there encouraging me.

Over the years I have had many encounters with the Irish Army and Navy because there have been divers from all over Ireland and further afield diving on OUR wreck without first of all contacting Desmond or myself. These divers had plundered much of *Laurentic's* valuable brass. The problems on the surface have been as many as those down below.

But once more, when I think of the gold, I am convinced it is there. But where? Where in the wreck is it?

A few years back after much research by my brother Eric, who brought over blueprints of the wreck, I was convinced the gold was in a certain area. But as Desmond and I studied the prints we began to realise we had been completely wrong. And what clinched it for me was while on a visit to Folkestone to see my

Ray Cossum and Eric Cossum with Ralph Williamson, a top diver, celebrate the recovery of a mass of salvage from *Laurentic* including portholes, 6" and 2·5" shells.

mother, Eric asked me if I would go with him to see Bill Mason, who we believed had died of the bends. Bill, I was glad to say, was very much alive although confined to a wheelchair. Diver Bill Mason had taken part in a great number of the world's greatest feats of salvage and he was one of the most modest and genuine gentlemen I have ever met. Bill had worked for that great salvage company, Risden and Beazly, who had made a short attempt for the rest of *Laurentic's* gold in 1952 but did not find any. Bill told us he had spoken to an old diver called Godfrey, a Durham man, who told him he had worked for the Mallet Company and they had recovered five bars of gold, but the company had gone bankrupt.

When we first purchased the *Laurentic*, Risden Beazly led us to believe that they owned her and that they intended to return to salvage her. We, of course, soon informed them that we were the owners and they should keep away. I don't believe they would have dived on the wreck if Godfrey had not convinced them that the gold was still there. When we were leaving Bill he told us he didn't believe the gold was there. But Eric, Desmond and myself did.

There have been many rumours about the gold and here are short accounts of two I have heard. This story was related to a friend of mine. His friend, one Alec Lyndsey, who originally came from Newtownstewart, worked in Derry in an antique shop in Shipquay Street owned by a Mr. Ross. Alec says that one day a sailor came into the antique shop carrying a brown paper parcel and asked Mr. Ross

Metal plates from gold area site on board the Consortium Recovery Ltd. ship *Holga Dane*.

would he be interested in buying some gold. According to Alec the parcel contained a bar of gold. He said the sailor was paid a sum of money and Alec remembers the gold being cut up in a small workshop at the back of the shop where he sometimes worked. A week later two detectives arrived and searched the shop and workshop. He believes one of the detectives was a man called Dykes. Alec remembers feeling the sweat bubbling on his brow as the detectives searched the workshop. Lying on the bench, in full view, was the very hacksaw that had been used to cut up the gold bar. The detectives missed it and went away.

The other story is about a freight yard at the bottom of the Strand Road. Apparently the big gate was held open by a block of black steel. One day as a horse and cart were driving into the yard the wheel of the cart caught the steel block and one of the workmen noticed the shine on the side of it. It turned out to be a gold bar with an "L" on it.

There is another story in a later chapter where gold was supposed to have been found. This was later turned into a television programme called, Confessions.

None of the above stories have been proven. The gold is still there and it was one of my ambitions to find it."

Many artifacts from the *Laurentic* adorn homes in the form of 6-inch shells as poker stands and portholes as mirrors but Mr. David Gilliland, a solicitor, once showed Ray a small table with a plaque in the middle of it. The plaque read, "This table was washed up from the wreck of the *Laurentic*." Mr. Gilliland believes it was washed up near Portsalon. The table had one leg missing when it was found. Later Mr. William Brown, a fisherman from Inch, with an extensive knowledge of the sea around Donegal, found the missing leg and apparently sold it for a "tanner" (sixpence - 2.5 new pence). Shortly after Mr. Gilliland acquired the four-legged table. It was when working for Mr. Gilliland that he was able to point out on the table the part where the extra leg had been fitted. The *Laurentic* table is supposed to be kept at Brook Hall in Culmore, Londonderry. Mr. Gilliland also told Ray that a relative of his was an officer guarding the defence boom between McCamish and Ned's Point and he would have been responsible for allowing the *Laurentic* in and out of the harbour at Buncrana on that fateful day.

Ray's first ambition has always been to find *Laurentic* gold but his other ambition was to take place on the surface of the water and bring him world-wide acclaim. Next he tells his story of some of his long distance swimming successes, in particular his gruelling swim across the English Channel.

CHAPTER FOUR

WE'LL MISS THE TIDE

"I was born in Folkestone (then a small town) on the South East Coast of Kent. My earliest memories of the English Channel were of the old fishermen I saw at the harbour every day on my way to school. Little did I think back then that the 21 mile stretch of water from England to France would play such an important part of my life. In the years to come not only would I swim it, I would work on the bottom as a diver. But the bug of long distance swimming would not affect me until 30 years later and not in my beloved hometown but in another country entirely.

Lough Swilly, known as the Lake of Shadows in County Donegal, Ireland, was a beautiful stretch of water on the north-west Atlantic coast. Like other holiday makers I would often visit the tiny seaside town of Buncrana for a picnic. I remember vividly one particular Sunday on such an outing wondering how long it would take a man to swim across to the other side. I soon dismissed the notion when I thought of how cold the water was. But the thought would not go away and the following Sunday I found myself, new bathing trunks and all, going in for a splash with the other holiday makers. Ten minutes later with my teeth chattering and my head pounding with the cold my first venture into long distance swimming ended. *Wise up Ray,* a tiny voice whispered, but a louder one would not go away. I looked across the Swilly to Rathmullan, a distance of five miles. I'll have to give this some serious thought if I'm going to swim from there to here. But where do I get information on long distance swimming?

It was to be another two years and a lot of training, both mentally and physically, before I stood on a beautiful July morning in my heavy cloth bathing shorts and a pair of Lone Ranger goggles with my boatman, Willie Brown, beckoning me to start or *"We'll miss the tide."* Shortly the gentle splash of oars and the occasional shout of encouragement from the boat was all I could hear. Two hours and fifteen minutes later I had achieved my first long distance swim of five miles from Rathmullan to Buncrana across Lough Swilly.

Back in 1964 long distance swimming in Ireland was unheard of and you were truly out on a limb, so when I staggered out of the water after my swim I was thunderstruck by the applause of the crowds of people who had gathered hoping to see me complete it. My cold shaking hands were grasped and squeezed and I thought - boy, now I've really got the bug.

Later, in 1966, I was to conquer that swim both ways non-stop in a time of 4 hours and 14 minutes. To this day no one else has attempted that exhausting double

Lough Swilly swim. Such are the tidal races that pilot and swimmer have to fully complete pre-swim planning and needless to say the weather plays the last card.

During that time I read over and over again two books which were presented to me. The first was called, "It's Cold in the Channel" by Sam Rocket. The other book was by Commander Gerald Forsberg O.B.E.R.N. (President of the Channel Swimming Association)- "Modern Long Distance Swimming".

My skill of long distance swimming came by trial and error and dare I say it an abundance of error.

On the first of June, 1970, I did another Lough Swilly swim. This time it was a 17-mile swim from Buncrana to Portsalon. My memory of that swim was the cold. Early in June is no time for such a long swim. No person has attempted that swim before, or since. At the finish I looked down to what I thought was about three feet of water. I stopped swimming to just walk out of the water. However, it was not 3 feet but more than 6 feet - so under I went. The crowd watching from Portsalon Pier thought I was about to drown. I was that cold I must have looked so pitiful that the lady who owned the local cafe/bar, Rita Smyth, took pity on me and gave me a tumbler of hot whiskey, and later I had a steaming hot bath. Dare I say it but the whiskey ended on the floor. Whiskey added to the mouthfuls of salt water I had swallowed during my swim do not mix.

Ray Cossum, John Hume, Tony O'Reilly, Des Cossum at the American Embassy, Dublin.

During my many distance swims I have had the feeling that this is what swimming is all about - survival of the sea and swimming from A to B, not just circuits of a swimming pool.

One of my early swims was from Portrush to Greencastle, from Northern Ireland to the Irish Republic, a distance of 19 miles. During this swim my pilot was in my debt, but not in the financial sense. Six months previously, during a bleak February day, he had caught his fishing nets on a wrecked submarine some 170 feet below the surface. He asked me would I dive and release the nets, which I duly did. To say it was a very dodgy job would be an understatement. The water was dark and I was surrounded by nets. To cut a long story short I did the job and my future pilot asked me, "How can I repay you?" I replied, "By piloting me on my next swim (the aforementioned Portrush to Greencastle swim) one day during the summer of 1967, naturally weather and tides permitting." Which he duly did and which I successfully completed. That pilot, John Henry Canning, later stated that he felt more afraid for me diving at that depth for his fishing nets than when he had been fishing through mine-fields during the war. Little did he know I was more scared than he was.

July 31st, 1970 - the day of my channel swim had arrived and I'll never forget it. After waiting for months for the right weather and tides, and training to keep in condition can be a trying time. But at last I had the word from my pilot. At that particular time he is your mentor. When he shouts "jump!" you feel like shouting back, "How High!"

By mid-afternoon I was laid out on one of the trawler's bunks and being told, "We will be off Cap-Priz-Nez in about two hours. Relax." Relax - how hard that was. As I lay there I tried to recall my well-meaning friends and relations telling me, "Ray, you can do it." But above those thoughts came the sound of the sea hitting the hull of the boat and the constant throb of the boat's propellers. It was a long two hours but then came the call down the hatch and my heart began pounding. "Ray, get ready! We're just approaching Cap-Priz-Nez." This was it. It was no longer a dream. This was for real. I was attempting to swim the English Channel. Many had tried and failed. Would I be one of them?

The row boat the trawler had been towing was pulled alongside as the pilot boat's engines stopped. My C.S.A. observer and the two members of the crew who were to row me the last few hundred yards through the shallow water boarded the row boat and we headed for shore. As we neared the beach I became suddenly aware it was thronging with hundreds of French holidaymakers. I felt a little embarrassed as I changed into my bathing trunks, cap and goggles while a curious horde of holidaymakers stood around me.

My C.S.A. observer had already briefed me and when the rowing boat pulled away from the beach he shouted, "Go!" Immediately he started his stopwatch. At 5.15 I waded past a number of people taking a dip and said, "Au Revoir" to the last couple and I was on my way. As I began swimming the boat was rowed out to the pilot boat again and tied to it. Shortly, with the pilot boat chugging along nearby, I was heading for England. For a few hundred yards the water was very shallow. At that point a thought crossed my mind. Maybe I could walk it. But soon the real swim began. It was a great relief, for at long last it was for real. I was really attempting a Channel swim.

Soon I was swimming alongside my pilot boat conscious now of my every move being watched. My swim had been well planned. Bert Read, the pilot of *The Accord* was just where we had agreed he would be. When I took the occasional glance up he was there just in the right position to keep his exhaust fumes from blowing into my face. I had agreed with Bert and the crew to chalk on a blackboard my stroke rate, the state of the tide and how long to go before I could get a plastic cup of beef tea. Soon it was being handed down to me on a net-ended stick. I took a quick few gulps to refresh myself making sure I did not touch the boat. That would have meant instant disqualification and all the preparations would have been for nothing.

Through the night my arms began to feel heavy. Torches were lit and a boom with a lamp attached to it was swung out over the side of the boat. This was so my crew could keep an eye on me just to confirm I was still in contact with my boat. As I swam that dark night my thoughts drifted to the *Laurentic*. Where was the gold? I knew it was there. These thoughts and the encouragement from the crew kept me going . "Ray, you're nearly there! Come on, keep swimming!" My arms were aching and felt like lead pipes and I was ice cold, but I kept going until at long last beautiful daylight began to appear.

Eventually we were approaching land and, though exhausted, I was glad to see the observer and two of the crew climb into the rowing boat. We where by then about a quarter of a mile from shore. I can still hear their shouts of encouragement. "Come on Ray, swim! Swim!" They shouted it over and over. Once I raised my head and shouted back, "What the */^** do you think I'm doing!" My mouth was as dry as toast and actually I must have been looking the worse for wear. Suddenly, before I knew it, my hands and feet were touching the sandy shore of East Wear Beach just east of Folkestone Harbour. The time was 6.56, the 1st. of August, and the rest is history.

Many times I have re-visited Folkestone. I still have a relative there and I often take a walk along 'The Lea's'. For anyone not familiar with Folkestone, it overlooks the Channel. As I stand there I can't quite take it in that I have swam all the way.

Des and Ray Cossum with Capt. Terence O'Neill, former Prime Minister of Northern Ireland.

Did I really work on the channel sea-bed as a diver? Did I, as a submariner, take passage through that same stretch of water? Did I then swim the same distance and then go right under both earth and water in La Shuttle? There must be a record there somewhere."

RAY'S SWIMS TO DATE.
Lough Swilly, County Donegal. (10 times) - 2 hours 15 minutes.
Double Lough Swilly - 4 hours 14 minutes.
Buncrana to Portsalon (17 miles) - 7 hours.
Portrush to Greencastle (19 miles) - 8 hours.
Across Lough Neagh, Northern Ireland - 6 hours.
Londonderry to Moville (20 miles) - 6 hours 51 minutes.
Rathlin to Ballycastle - 3 hours.
Fain Head to Ballycastle - 2 hours 30 minutes.
Belfast Lough (twice) - 4 hours.
Lake Windermere - 7 hours 35 minutes.

One of Ray's proudest achievements was when, with his son Des, he coached and trained the Irish Junior English Channel relay team that broke the World Record for the fastest junior team crossing in 1978. That record still stands today.

West of Ireland. In 1971, 13 members of the club made history when they found the Spanish Armada wreck, *La Trinidad Valencera.*

In the early years, when few people were diving, Ray was often called on to take part in many searches for people lost at sea. Below is a letter from the Garda Siochana to the Head Postmaster at the Post Office in Derry, where Ray worked, acknowledging his help.

Mr. Barker,

Head Postmaster,

G.P.O. Londonderry.

Dear Mr. Barker,

On behalf of the District Force, and on my own behalf, I would like to thank you and through you, Mr. Cossum, who I understand is a Post Office employee, for the very great trouble and expense to which the latter went while searching for the body of the late Garda Joseph A.Grennan, who was drowned at Fahan on 13th. Inst.

The mother of the dead member was well aware of the help rendered by Mr. Cossum and she has since asked me to convey her thanks and that of her family to him. As she herself put it, "Everybody was wonderful. The divers risked their lives to find my poor son's body."

Our own Sub Aqua Club members were also high in their praise at the assistance they got from Mr. Cossum when it came to advice, replenishing the air supply in their breathing apparatus etc. and they have also requested me to tender through you their very sincere thanks for all that was done for them.

Very Sincerely

Superintendent (D. Friel)

Ray was also voted North-West Sportsman of the Year - the first Englishman to hold the title. "The award goes to a man who achieved something that relatively few men the world over could have done."

Ray was in the Royal Navy for 8 years, 5 years in R.N. Submarine Service with part of his submarine service as a Submarine Escape Instructor. He has also worked as a commercial diver which included rig diving in the North Sea and world wide salvage diving, cargo and wreck recovery.

CHAPTER FIVE
"FREELANCE SCAVENGERS"

Ray recalls their first efforts at salvaging the *Laurentic*. "In 1969 we bought a 12-foot C craft inflattable with a 12-horsepower outboard engine. We were crazy to even think of going out to the wreck in such a small craft but in those early days perhaps being crazy helped. Our equipment, to say the least, was very basic. Besides having no compass, no G.P.S. (as they hadn't been invented), and no ship-to-shore radio, we didn't even tell anyone of our plans. All we had were the vague land fixes of where the big L was and a mad determination to dive her. Even our diving equipment was mostly home-made by Eric. His suit, harness, you name it, my brother made it. Eric even built our compressor from spare air-craft parts. The filters on the compressor, which were able to stand up to 2,000 p.s.i., were made from air-craft spares and the fear of the compressor blowing up was always in our minds. The noise of the compressor sounded like it was crushing stones and many times it broke down resulting in weeks without a dive. Such were the early days of our diving. I am sure such a small craft has never made so lonesome a trip. It took all our guts and blind faith to venture out into the Atlantic so far from land.

I remember one particular day, when on our way out on our flimsy inflatable, the sea suddenly grew dark. My diving companion, Tony Devine, shouted to me above the sound of the crashing waves, "Go back! For God's sake Ray, go back!" We were just in time and with the monstrous black waves chasing us we managed to get to the safety of Portsalon Pier. I remember Tony telling me he was sick with fear and that he "was never so frightened in his life." That experience made me think twice and from then on I checked the weather before venturing out again. Along with Tony and the late Martin McCourt we often made the long haul out to the wreck site. Huge waves had by now become our welcome in the site area. They seemed to say, *"I dare you to defy us."*

Back then our method of salvaging the brass and copper was as follows: when we were sure the marks were in line and the *Laurentic* was beneath us a shot line attached to a four-stone weight was dropped. Other lines were dropped too. These were there to haul up any portholes or other brass and copper we could tie on. When the sea was choppy it was quite a task getting our scuba-gear on and many a time we were almost pitched out of the boat.

One disastrous salvage effort which I'll never forget was my intention to salvage a 3-ton gun metal pump. I intended to lift the pump using a 5-ton lifting bag. When it was on the surface and tied to the inflatable it was then to be towed to Buncrana - 20 miles away. When I think about it now I must have been mad. Even as we headed out I had a feeling it was going to end in disaster. That day Dessie and a friend of his from Antrim, Stewert Taylor, accompanied me. Stewert was originally from Manchester and he had assured us he was a top diver and wanted us to give him a trial.

It took us 4 hours to reach the wreck site from Buncrana but shortly I was heading down the shotline pulling the heavy lifting bag after me. It was a hard struggle, and I was using my air quickly. By the time I reached the pump and began to tie the bag to it I was nearly out of air. Realising that Stewert could probably tie on the rest of the straps I surfaced. I looked around. It was getting quite choppy. I quickly told Stewert what I wanted him to do. I could see he was nervous, yet he went below. When he came up a few minutes later he told me he had not managed to secure the bag as safely as he wanted so, using what air he had left, I dropped below. In three minutes I had the pump secured to the bag and seconds later I was venting air from my mouthpiece into it. Shortly the bag, with the pump attached, was heading to the surface. Luckily it stayed there. It was now past mid-day. My worst nightmare was in front of me. As I started up the engine and Dessie and Stewert secured the bag with the pump to the inflatable I could feel my heart pounding. The tide was too strong. I knew the small engine wasn't powerful enough to tow the heavy pump and bag all the way to Buncrana but, after a few hours, we were just bearing into the entrance to Lough Swilly.

Around 7pm a cruiser, *The Maid of Crana,* arrived and towed us on into the Swilly until near midnight, then headed back out to sea. Around two in the morning we were abreast of Buncrana Pier when our engine stopped. Immediately we began to drift back out. After a few frantic efforts to restart the engine I knew there was nothing for it, so I entered the dark water and began to swim for the pier. As I swam I cursed myself for my stupidity. But in the darkness I saw a cabin crew who had been at a party in the Harbour Bar getting ready to take a run around the harbour. I shouted to them and luckily they heard me. A couple of minutes later I was picked up. Shortly we were pulling up along Buncrana Pier. It was a sore lesson and one I never forgot.

For the next couple of years there was very little could stop me diving on the *Laurentic.* The lure of the gold was so strong. Many a time we returned to port with my tiny craft filled to the top with portholes and other brass artifacts, but no gold. By then my son Desmond was diving with me. Occasionally my other son, Grahame would come with us.

In the early seventies Ray did many dives with Eric, Des and others on the *Laurentic.* By then Ray knew every part of the wreck but there was still no sign of the gold, only a few silver coins that were scattered about the gold area. But disturbing news was coming to Ray that unauthorised divers were diving on the wreck. And worse - these modern day pirates were lifting valuable pieces of scrap brass ie; portholes, 6-inch shells etc. from her. Diving teams, and even small salvage companies, were stealing the *Laurentic's* artifacts and Ray realised he had to do something. He couldn't watch the wreck all the time. It was suggested to Ray that he write to The Irish Minister of Defence and the Marine explaining his predicament.

Around that time a letter appeared in the local newspaper.

OWNERS OF FAMOUS SWILLY WRECK.

DERRY DEEP-SEA DIVERS WANT PROTECTION FROM "PIRATES"

A Derry father and son who are the official owners of a famous wreck off the Donegal coast have condemned the operations of what they call "Freelance scavengers" and have launched a campaign to get the maritime laws changed to provide them with more protection.

Ray and Des Cossum with the bell of the *Laurentic* during the salvage operation on *Allerton*, 1979.

Deep-sea divers, Raymond Cossum and his son, Dessie, bought the salvage rights five years ago of the Belfast built liner LAURENTIC which was sunk by a German U-boat off Malin Head in 1917. The *Laurentic* was carrying £5 million in gold bullion when she went down. All but 20 of the gold ingots were recovered in a 7-year salvage operation which is included in the Guinness Book of Records. These 20 ingots are almost certainly at the bottom of Lough Swilly. Under the salvage rights they purchased from the Government five years ago the Cossums are entitled to the valuable non-ferrous scrap metal which they reckon is worth £80,000 alone. Under the agreement with the British Treasury, they will get 90 percent of

The bow bell in the church tower at Portsalon.

the value of any gold they bring up. And at present rates each of the 20 bars is worth about £80,000. The Cossums say, "We are primarily interested in the scrap, but if we find the gold as well so much the better. And we also believe there is a fortune in unrecovered silver florins down there."

"A DISGRACE"

But unauthorised divers, they say, are presenting them with a problem. "They are going down and bringing up scrap metal which is our property. We have spent a lot of money and a lot of time doing exploratory work and finding out what is there. We know who is doing it and we will have no hesitation in getting court orders against them. We have impounded scrap which people have taken and we will do it again.

"It's a disgrace," they say. "And it's happening to other wrecks as well."

The Cossums are trying to get some of the other professional diving syndicates together to bring pressure on the Government for a change in what they describe as the antiquated maritime laws. Raymond suggests that no divers should be allowed on any wreck without first getting permission from the owner and then informing the nearest police station, which could be supplied with a list of local wrecks and their owners. The police should also be authorised to prevent divers landing scrap until they could prove ownership.

"PIRACY"

"Operations by freelance divers in shallow waters has become rife," he says. "And it is considered a bonanza. This would not be allowed in any other sphere of operations."

And Dessie says, "What's going on at the moment amounts to a kind of modern day piracy on the high seas."

The Cossums said that sub-aqua clubs are helping by telling their members to stay away from the *Laurentic*.

A Department of Trades spokesman said the wreck was not covered by any of their legislation. If the owners wanted to stop the activities of other divers they had to seek an injunction from the courts.

"We are only concerned with wrecks of historical or archaeological interest," he said.

But Raymond Cossum replies - "Why should the legitimate owner have the expense and frustration of legal action, sometimes very costly, in order to stop this plunder?"

ANOTHER WRECK

The Cossums are also interested in the battleship *Audacious,* which ran into a German mine during exercises in Tory Sound in Octobe, 1914. She was taken in tow by the White Star Liner *Olympic* but sank when she got close to the Swilly.

Regarding the *Laurentic,* Raymond told a "Journal" reporter that a Dutch-American salvage concern, which specialised in the recovery of treasure, is interested in carrying out a survey of the *Laurentic* from the treasure aspect. Raymond incidentally has just returned to Derry after a spell of deep-sea diving off the North-Sea oil rigs. Before that he was in the Far East and plans to return there shortly. While in Derry he is training at the City swimming baths for his planned two-way Channel swim.

(ends)

Through Ray badgering the authorities about illegal salvage new laws were brought into force. In 1993 the Merchant Shipping (Salvage and Wreck) Act stated that:

A person shall be guilty of an offence if, in relation to a wrecked or stranded vessel or other wreck, such person-

(a) Impedes or hinders or attempts to impede or hinder the saving thereof;

(b) Conceals any wreck;

(c) Obliterates any mark on wreck;

(d) Wrongfully carries away or removes any wreck or;

(e) Interferes with any wreck in any way.

1. If a Judge of the District Court is satisfied by information on oath of a member of the Garda Siochana or a receiver that there is reasonable cause for suspecting that any wrecked or stranded vessel or other wreck is being concealed by or is in the possession of some person who is not the owner or receiver of it or is otherwise being improperly dealt with, the judge may issue a search warrant under this section.

2. A search warrant issued under this section shall be expressed and operate to authorise a named member of the Garda Siochana or a named receiver, accompanied by such members of the Garda Siochana and officers of Customs and Excise as the named member or receiver thinks necessary, at any time or times within one month from the date of issue of the warrant, on production if so requested of the warrant -

(a) To enter (if necessary by force) the land, premises, vehicle, vessel or aircraft named in the warrant,

(b) To search the land, premises, vehicle, vessel or aircraft and any persons found therein,

(c) To examine anything found therein,

(d) If there is reasonable ground for suspecting that any thing-

(i) May be required as evidence in proceedings for an offence under this part,

(ii) Should be in the possession of the receiver for retention or disposal in accordance with the provisions of this Part, to seize and detain such thing.

But the above law was to come much later. In 1978, fearing that the gold would be stolen, Eric wrote to the Treasury Solicitor with regard to confirming their ownership and re-negotiating their entitlement to the gold, finding out its proper value and also to inform the Treasury of the Cossum Syndicate's intention of contacting a commercial salvage company with an interest in Salvaging the *Laurentic*.

Holy Head salvage platform over *Laurentic*. Raking through sea bed debris for coins and pieces of gold are: (l to r) Ralph Williamson, Jack Frost, (divers) two members of tug crew, Paddy Kelly (crane driver), Ray Cossum (owner), Frank Mausly (operations manager).

On the 22nd. February 1978 Eric received a reply.

The Treasury Solicitor

Mathew Parker Street,

London, SW1H9NN.

Dear Mr. Cossum,

THE LAURENTIC

Further to this matter, I am pleased to inform you that I have now received a reply with regard to your queries. Briefly, I am instructed that the current international rules affecting gold purchased by central banks would not permit the Bank of England to pay more than £14.5833 per fine troy ounce for gold. However, you are no doubt aware that these rules are expected to come to an end within the next few months and the bank of England expects to be free to determine its own buying price.

The current open market price for gold, which I assume may well be the new official price, is approximately £90 per fine troy ounce. Having regard to your request to re-negotiate your agreement, I am prepared to recommend such re-negotiations and assuming that the price of gold remains at about £90 per fine troy ounce, I suggest that it would not be unreasonable for the proceeds of the gold recovered to be shared equally between yourselves and the Treasury. If such were adopted I anticipate any potential recoveries will realise 3 and 4 times the sum envisaged when your agreement was signed in 1969. Having regard to the above, I shall be glad to hear further from you and I trust that the information contained will assist you in possibly reaching some agreement in obtaining assistance to effect recovery of the gold remaining on board, or in the vicinity of the LAURENTIC.

I look forward to hearing from you.

Yours Sincerely

D A Stalker

For the Treasury Solicitor

Included with the letter was the following:-

THE OLD DOLLAR I.M.F. RATE, AND WHICH IS STILL THE SAME UNTIL APRIL 1978. AND TO REMEMBER THE ABOVE DOLLAR RATE WAS THE ONE THAT RIZDEN BEAZLEY MARINE LTD. DIDN'T LIKE BECAUSE IT WAS /S/ 42 PER FINE TROY OUNCE OF GOLD. (which is near £21 per fine troy ounce of gold)

THE OLD DOLLAR /S/ I.M.F. RATE.

(1) £21 PER FINE TROY OUNCE OF GOLD.

(2) £336 PER FINE TROY POUND OF GOLD.

(3) £8,400 PER FINE INGOT OF GOLD.

(4) £184,800 FOR 20 INGOTS OF GOLD.

(5) And to share equally with the TREASURY SOLICITOR (THE BANK OF ENGLAND) The sum is then £92,400.

THE NEW BANK OF ENGLAND POUND RATE FROM APRIL 1978, WHEN THE I.M.F. RATE IS THEN PAID OFF.

THE NEW POUND RATE FROM APRIL 1978.

(1) £90 PER FINE TROY OUNCE OF GOLD.

(2) £1,440 PER FINE TROY POUND OF GOLD.

(3) £36,000 FOR ONE INGOT OF GOLD.

(4) £792,000 PER 20 INGOTS OF GOLD.

(5) And to share equally with THE TREASURY SOLICITOR (THE BANK OF ENGLAND) The sum is then £396,000.

I will get in touch with Risden and Beazley Marine Ltd. and find the figure which should their company carry out the gold recovery, if and when they go ahead, I will get in touch with our Solicitor in Folkestone, he will then get in touch with the Treasury Solicitor.

CHAPTER SIX

THE TALE OF ANOTHER LAURENTIC BELL

After searching the wreck for another year the Cossums decided to contact a group of business men who had advertised their salvage services. The vessel they used was supposed to be a First World War tank carrier. Ray remembers that disastrous season vividly.

Salvage vessel *Allerton* at mooring Portsalon,
Lough Swilly 1979.

"We nicknamed the salvage ship the M.V. *Allerton*, "The Black Pig." (for those familiar with Captain Pugwash). A couple of months after contacting the business directors of the salvage company we arranged to meet them at the Dunadry Hotel in Antrim to thrash out terms. In the main it was decided for payment towards search and recovery of the gold the directors would receive the value of whatever scrap they could raise. And it was agreed the *Allerton* and her diving crew were to arrive in Portsalon four weeks later.

I'll never forget that long wait on Portsalon Pier for the arrival of the ship. When I saw the salvage outfit I couldn't believe my eyes. There was no crane, no decompression tank, and the vessel looked more like a hulk than a proper sea going craft. I wondered how it had managed to stay afloat on the journey from England.

After a few minutes a tiny inflatable was lowered from it and headed towards the pier. When its occupants landed Des and I were introduced to the skipper, his brother, the diver and his 16-year-old son. To say the least we were stunned - one diver and no equipment to talk of. The diver introduced himself as Victor Cowan Dickie. Now Vic was not your average guy. He was well over 6 foot 4 inches and built like Hercules. He told us he was a Scot, with an English education and he had been in the S.A.S. He also told us his grandfather was Gordon of Khartoum. I believed him because he exuded so much self-confidence I was overwhelmed. Vic's son was over 6 foot. His wife and daughter were to arrive a couple of weeks later.

But down to the salvage work. At first we were reluctant to go out to the site but Vic soon persuaded us everything would work out well for us. To say Vic was like an underwater vacuum cleaner with regard to finding brass and copper would be an understatement. Pieces of brass and copper we had passed over for years without seeing seemed to leap into his arms. Vic was able to hone in on the non-ferrous metal like no one I've ever seen. He also had a violent temper.

One day he came up from a dive, pulled off his diving set, and crashed it hard on the deck. Roaring like a madman he demanded certain size shackles and slings to recover more scrap. We 'bravely' pointed out that he had used up all his dive time. Vic took no notice and as he pulled on a set he tried to explain above the noise of his son's Ghetto Blaster that he was working on his own dive tables. As he was speaking his son turned up the sound of the music. With a snarl Vic tore the blaster from him and smashed it to pieces on the deck. Then, without a lifejacket or buckling his harness, he grabbed the wire and leapt over the bows. Already kitted up for my dive, I followed him. On the way down he let go of the down line and the next thing I saw was Vic crashing onto the wreck in a cloud of rust and metal. Shortly more scrap was on its way up. I've dived with many good salvage divers but not one of them could keep up with Vic. He was breaking all the rules and not doing enough decompression stops. But week after week he seemed to be getting away with it.

Then came a day I'll never forget. I had to go into Derry on business and Des was to stay with the operation to make sure salvage work would run as smoothly as Vic would let it. When I returned early afternoon I met Des and Vic. They were smiling. Des told me Vic had found the *Laurentic* bell and the telegraph. I foolishly said, "Rubbish. There was only one bell on the *Laurentic* and the Royal Navy found it in 1924." But when they showed me the bell I was stunned. Apparently Des and Vic had found the bell which had hung in the bridge area of the great ship. The other bell, which hangs in Portsalon church, was from the bows. Vic apparently had seen the edge of the bell sticking out of the sea-bed near the wreck. I began to wonder how we had missed it. We had dived many times on the wreck as had many other divers and no one had seen the bell. It was easy now to understand how we had missed the gold. I was even more convinced the gold was still there.

That evening, on Vic's last dive, and as he was removing his diving equipment, he collapsed on deck. I had continually warned him he must be in cahoots with the devil to have gotten away with his dangerous disregard for proper dive tables for so long. After examining him the skipper said Vic was in a bad way. Then we realised the ship's radio wasn't working. It took us quite a while to get the 18-stone Vic into the inflatable and quickly we headed for Portsalon Pier. When we reached it I ran to phone for help. Unfortunately the Irish Air Rescue service were engaged in a sea rescue somewhere else but they put us in contact with their British counterparts. Two-and-a-half hours later a Royal Marine Helicopter was circling around the Pier. It circled several times checking us out, then landed in front of the Portsalon Hotel a couple of hundred yards away. Immediately I ran towards them. When I got there the crew would not come out. This was during the Troubles and naturally they were suspicious of us. The pilot shouted to me, "We do not leave the Chopper! You bring the injured man to us!" By then a couple of hundred people had gathered around Vic, who still lay on the inflatable as white as a ghost, and for all we knew was dying. We eventually asked a few men to help us carry Vic and the inflatable to the helicopter. Shortly, with Vic and his wife on board, the helicopter headed for the decompression chamber at Craigavon, in Northern Ireland.

The doctor who examined Vic stated later that his blood had a head on it like a pint of Guinness. Vic was put into the decompression chamber on Sunday night and came out again at 2 am on Monday morning. He was discharged a few days later and arrived back in Portsalon with his wife, daughter, son and two of the salvage company's directors. In the Portsalon Hotel Vic's son apologised to me. I asked him what for? He motioned towards one of the windows in the hotel and said he had come close to throwing the two directors out of it. I asked him why? He said the directors had docked him a day's pay for visiting his father in hospital. After that things came to a quick end. Des and I had a meeting with the directors and we agreed the show was over. It was decided we would have the *Laurentic* bell and a few other artifacts and the directors would have the hold full of scrap. To me the bell was of greater value than the scrap.

When the directors left, Vic wanted to take over the *Allerton* and go back out to the *Laurentic*. We refused. Vic later wrote to me telling me he hoped to return with a suitable salvage vessel and try again. It never happened.

The following day Des and I examined the bell in greater detail. We had noticed the clapper was missing. I had found out that when the ship put to sea the clapper on the bridge bell is removed until the bell is to be used for watches (shifts, in marine terms). We had also noticed that there were a great many indents on the outside of the bell. It was as though it had been struck by a hammer or something hard. Only an emergency, such as the ship sinking, would have left the ship's bell in that condition. The clapper was probably locked away at that time.

We kept the bell for a short time but later thought it would be nice for other people to see it, so a friend of mine, and a master salvager of great renown, bought it and took it to London. Paul Rowlands, who was a director with Euro Salv. told me his father, Tim Rowlands, had loaned the bell to a company that later went into liquidation and the bell disappeared."

Ray finishes by saying, "In hindsight I should have held onto the bell. It would have been nice to have donated it to our own local museum. If anyone out there knows where the *Laurentic* bridge bell is please return it to me."

Des and Ray Cossum with the missing bell.

Realising the law was not fully on their side with regards to illegal diving on the *Laurentic,* and that there was a danger of one of the pirates finding the gold, the Cossums sought the help of another salvage company. This was one they knew had the equipment and credentials. After a meeting with his brother Eric and Desmond, it was decided that they go in with "Holyhead Towing Co. Ltd."

In 1984 the Holyhead Company began operations. Captain F.P. Mawdlely and his team of divers excavated an area on the sea bed of rock and

Salvage barge being towed by the *Afon Goch* heading to *Laurentic.*

shingle 40 feet by 60 feet to a depth of 18 feet. They did what "Damant" and his team had already done before, hoping that he had overlooked a few bars.

THE FOLLOWING EQUIPMENT WAS USED

Tug: *Afon Gough* Lloyd's 100 A1 classed for coastal and middle trade waters. 18-tons BP, 1200-BHP, twin screws in fixed knozzles and rudders.

FLAT TOP PONTOON - 75 ft X 45 ft X 9ft depth, class for coastal operation. 4 X 5-ton winches with 4 suitable anchor buoys and 4 wires to lay a 4 point system.

1 X 5-ton winch, if necessary for other requirements other than moorings.

45-ton Crawler Crane with grab, mounted and fixed to pontoon.

2-man decompression chamber with equipment.

Compressor, air-lift and hose.

DIVERS: Team of 4 divers and supervisor, based on 10 hours per day.

PORTAKABIN AND GENERATOR.:

Total period of 30 days from departure of Holyhead to arrival back to Holyhead.

But because of the bad weather and after 30 days they finished operations and returned to Holyhead without recovering any gold. They did however amongst other artifacts salvage one of Laurentic's six inch guns.

The next company the Cossum Syndicate went in with was Consortium Recovery Ltd. The Cossum Syndicate deeded the rights of the *Laurentic* to Consortium Recovery Ltd for the sum of £16,666.66 each (£50,000) divided between Ray, his brother and Desmond. Below is a copy of one of the complicated agreements between the Cossums and Consortium Recovery.

The Agreement:

Consortium Salvage Ltd. of: 134 Lots Road, London
(C.S.) of the one part: and

Eric Cossum of 2 Boulogne Court, Harbour Way, Folkestone, Kent. ("Consultant") of the other part.

Whereas:

1. By an agreement dated 21st April, 1969 ("Contract"), the Ministry of Defence transferred its ownership of the wreck of the S.S. *Laurentic* ("Wreck") to Consultant subject to a retained interest over any gold or silver recovered from the wreck ("Cargo").

2.   C.S. is a company specialising in subsea cargo recoveries:

3.   C.S. and Consultant have agreed to collaborate in endeavoring to recover the cargo in the following terms:

THE PARTIES AGREE AS FOLLOWS:

1.   (a) C.S. confirms that title to the wreck is held by Consultant.

(b) Consultant confirms that for the duration of this agreement:

(a) His permission is granted to C.S. to work on the wreck.

(b) He will provide all his knowledge and experience and undertakes that Raymond and Desmond Cossum will provide all their knowledge and experience, concerning the wreck and its cargo to C.S.

2.   (a) All operations will be at the risk and cost of C.S. and shall also be under the control and planning of C.S. as shall the security measures to be adopted with regard to any of the wreck and/or cargo recovered.

(b) net revenue received from the sale of any of the wreck and/or cargo recovered by operations conducted under or during this agreement shall be divided as follows:

C.S.   % of net revenue

Consultant   % of net revenue

Net revenue shall be the reveue received from the sale of cargo after deduction of:

1. The entitlement of the government under the contract.

2.   "Project costs" being the charges and or interests of third party suppliers of equipment, services and or finance and:

3.   Any taxes or duties imposed by the Irish or U.K. Authorities.

C.S. shall keep proper books of account and records showing all transactions relating to the establishment of project costs.

3.   The agreement shall continue until 30 days after either party receives from the other notice of termination issued on any of the following grounds:

(a) If no recovery operations are undertaken during 1985 or if no further operations are undertaken during any subsequent calendar year. In such case C.S. shall not from the date of termination involve themselves in any further operations on the wreck whether by finance, operations or otherwise except with the consent of Consultant.

(b) If any of the Consultants knowledge is withheld from C.S. or incorrect, or if the contract is withdrawn or for any reason invalid, Consultant shall not from the date of termination involve themselves in any activities related to the recovery of the cargo whether by research, finance, operations or otherwise without making provision for the recovery of any Project Costs which have not been recovered from sale of cargo recovered under this agreement except with the consent of Consultant.

1.   All information of the proprietary nature obtained by one of the party from the other shall be held on a confidential basis.

2.   Consultant shall not publish or permit to be published or supplied to any news media any information about the subject matter of this agreement (nor any business of C.S. generally) without the written consent of C. S. Such consent shall apply to that specific application and shall set no precedent.

3.   The parties shall have joint rights over revenue received from any book or film concerning the Laurentic and its cargo and shall share all such revenue and meet all such costs equally. The provisions of clause 3 shall remain binding notwithstanding the termination of this agreement.

4.   I, C.S. shall have the power to assign the benefit of this agreement to any subsidiary, affiliated or otherwise associated company to any joint venture (or participant therein) or principle contractor which may be involved with the subject matter to which this agreement relates.

5.   1. This agreement:

(a) Constitutes the entire agreement between the parties on the subject to which it relates and supersedes all prior negotiations, representations and agreements.

(b) Shall only be modified or otherwise amended by a document duly executed on behalf of both parties.

(c) Shall be interpreted by application of English Law.

5. 2.   Nothing in this agreement or in the relationship of its parties shall be constructed as in any sense creating a partnership between the parties, or as giving to any party any of the rights, or subjecting any party to any of the liabilities, of a partner.

6. Any notice under this agreement shall be in writing and addressed to:

Consortium Salvage Limited.
134, Lots Road, London, SW100RJ.
Telex: 893851 WRENST G.

E. Cossum,
2, Boulogne Court, Harbour way,
Folkestone, Kent, CT20 1QP.

Notices shall be effective:

If delivered by hand at time of delivery:
If sent by telex, telegram or cable, at the time of receipt.
If sent by prepaid registered mail 5 days after the time of mailing.

IN WITNESS OF THIS AGREEMENT C.S. have caused it to be executed on its behalf by its duly authorised officer, and Consultant has executed it in person, the executed agreement being in two originals.

CONSORTIUM SALVAGE LIMITED.

CONSULTANT.

The following Operating Plan will give a good example of how much work went into the Consortium Recovery's salvage operation. Using the *Holga Dane*, an impressive working vessel, their plan, based originally on 21 days' work, was to create reasonable extensions to "Damant's" excavation, moving forward and aft and inboard. It was not important where the starting point was located and this decision was made after a survey of the site. The position they chose was the most accessible, readily identifiable section from a chosen corner, forward and inward.

Salvage vessel *Holga Dane* over *Laurentic*.

The rate of progress throughout had been good but the weather was not kind for the first 12 days on site. The wind remained northwest between Force 4 and 8. Although they lost one day off site and only one day off site for weather, progress was slowed by the necessity for repairing damage to equipment resulting from the heavy swell. Hoses and cables for the air-lift, water blasters and cutting gear, were the most affected.

The vessel maintained station well considering that for one continuous period of three days they were waist deep over the stern without stopping operations. Some deck crew managed to make running repairs and the time loss was kept to a minimum possible in the circumstances.

There were a number of slight deviations to the workscope as originally planned. These came about for a number of reasons, but all relate to fresh knowledge gathered in the course of the work. As a result of these deviations and the few extra bell runs achieved before the work ceased, more area was covered than was originally envisaged.

The first significant change relates to the after-side of the excavation. Precise measurement is always difficult for a single diver over a great length. As plates were moved the new exposed edges were fixed by measurements and were double checked. Findings confirmed that the bullion room and first-class saloon lay closer to the forward end of the excavation than originally estimated and that "Damant" had, in fact, moved further aft than appears practical. For this reason less work was done extending the excavation astern and instead more work was undertaken in extending forward.

Upon removing plates around the line of portholes on the after side of the excavation, and clearing the sea bed below, the divers found that the black concretion resulting from the wreck, continued forward through the area excavated by "Damant". It was, therefore, decided to continue excavating the sea bed across the full width of "Damant's" area as it appears that the work was not originally carried out with sufficient care to guarantee total clearance of the area.

The net effect of the reducing work in the after area and adding 3.2.1. and 3.2.1. above, was a net increase in the workscope of seven days but better progress along the turn of the bilge allowed us to complete the full workscope in four days over the schedule.

But after all the work Consortium Recovery Ltd. found no gold. This company did intend to return but were unable to do so.

One diver who worked with Consortium Recovery, Adam Ridge, remembers he had the last dive on the *Laurentic* before salvage was to finish. "We had all worked hard and we were all going to have a few souvenirs to take home. Up until now we had not moved from the work area.

Everyone had walked to the ends of their umbilicals and cleaned the whole area of everything that shone.

I started my dive just after mid-night. As usual the visibility was excellent. Looking up I could see the lights of the *Holga Dane* 40m above. I crossed over three propshafts and on reaching the starboard side I began to work my way north, climbing through the engine room and heading towards the bows.

Above me the ship followed on my command. Progress was slow, as I determined to leave as little as possible behind. Hanging from the crane was a large work basket which I kept level with me for the whole dive. As soon as I found something of value it was only a few feet and I could throw it into the skip.

Portholes came off with not too much trouble (a 38mm spanner soon had the brass nuts flying!). Once the nuts were removed you could drive a chisel under the edge of the porthole, jam in a six-foot crowbar with a sharp tug upwards and that was it - about ten minutes was average.

Ray Cossum on the bridge of the salvage vessel *Holga Dane*.

Still working my way forward I found myself in the magazine. Rack upon rack of shells of all sizes. I filled two baskets full before the deck crew decided we had got enough. As I got nearer to the bows there was less damage to the ship. The bows were intact with some wood still left on the deck and rails around the gunnels. I now headed south down the port side and soon came across the anchor winches, quickly followed by the forward mast.

Soon after this was an area of portholes, dozens of them, so I set to work. By now I had been out of the bell for a little over four hours and dawn was beginning to break. As I worked the sun began to climb and I became more aware of my surroundings. In the early morning gloom a shape was unfolding to the south of me. It was time to explore further. I was well and truly bored with portholes.

I moved towards what turned out to be one of *Laurentic's* huge guns pointing towards the surface and looking in remarkably good condition. Thirty feet away I could see another. Moving on, with visibility increasing rapidly, I saw more portholes and then brass windows. These were loose and there seemed to be dozens of them. It became clear I was standing at the edge of a collapsed bridge and the windows outlined the boundary.

I headed towards the centre of the Bridge. The *Laurentic's* telegraph had taken a hammering over the years, but it was coming home with me. After eight hours in the water I had walked right around the *Laurentic*. We had all the goodies we wanted. It was time to call it a day.

My decompression took three days."

When the *Holga Dane* and her salvage crew left, Ray realised that they had done their best to find the gold. But now the Revenue and Customs began to be concerned about who owned the wreck and, if any of the gold was found, who owned it.

This fax was sent to Mr. Ted Mc Laughlin, Revenue and Customs, Letterkenny, Co. Donegal from Consortium Recovery Ltd.

Dear Mr. McLaughlin,

RE-WRECK OF "LAURENTIC".

Last week you spoke to one of my colleagues in Aberdeen, Derek Evans, as a result of which we thought it would be helpful, and hopefully save further problems, if I confirmed the current status of the wreck.

The wreck is owned by Consortium Recovery Ltd, who purchased it from the Cossum brothers, also the Cossum brothers still own a share when the gold is discovered, with the active approval and involvement of H.M. Treasury in the UK. Since then the company has mounted extensive operations on the wreck and have found nothing of value.

The depth of the wreck means that for safe and sustained working, reasonable sophisticated equipment is required, some of which can be accessed through an allied company, Underwater Excavation Ltd., with the majority being for outside supply source from the North Sea oil industry.

Being a cyclical industry, there are periods where such an operation becomes more cost effective than at other times. However, the opportunity is always under surveillance and hopes of eventually retrieving some benefit for past effects has never been abandoned.

In the meantime Mr. Ray Cossum, who we believe is already known to your office, keeps a watching brief. He is the wreck site area manager on his and our behalf, accordingly whilst we have no objection to recreational diving on the wreck providing those involved do so at their own risk and have declared themselves to Mr. Ray Cossum, we would, as a matter of course, advise your office if a recovery operation was planned which was authorised by ourselves.

If you require any further information, or for any other reason wish to contact the company, please do not have any hesitation in contacting myself, John Clarke, Derek Evans or Ray Cossum, at the Aberdeen office shown below.

Yours Sincerely

Nicholes Sinclair Brown

Copy Ray Cossum.

In the circumstances it was decided later to dissolve Consortium Recovery Ltd. Later Eric received a letter from Consortium Recovery Ltd.

Nicholas Sinclair-Brown

Baldwin Barn

Swaffham Prior,

Cambridgeshire, CB5 OLD

Dear Eric,

THE LAURENTIC

I have discussed the matter of above with John Clarke and Nick Sills. Both Nick and John were, until recently, executive directors of a sub sea company in Aberdeen which allowed them to monitor and organise opportunities to resume work on the *Laurentic*. This is no longer the case, and in the circumstances it has been decided to dissolve Consortium Recovery Ltd. As I understand from the Company's Registrar, this will take about five months to complete and any assets then in the company will belong to the Treasury Solicitor.

It is our general wish to provide you with as much flexibility as is practicable to pursue your own ideas regarding the *Laurentic*. Accordingly both John and Nick have signified their readiness to the Company signing a waiver, release, transfer or other document in your favour if this would be helpful to you. The relationship developed over the years means that no payment would be expected, but it would be up to you to prepare any relevant documentation.

Both Nick and John have considerable experience relating to the wreck and work conducted on it. Accordingly you may wish to discuss with them the possibility of their acting as consultants. if so please let me know and I will let you have their telephone numbers.

In the meantime please give some thought to the above and let me know if there are any steps you wish to be taken.

Kind regards

Nick Sinclair-Brown

Eric then received another letter with the document of transfer from Consortium Recovery Ltd.

Consortium Recovery Ltd.

Swaffham Priory,

Cambridgeshire, CB5 OLD.

Dear Eric,

The document of transfer is enclosed and has been redrafted to provide separately for the *Laurentic* and the obligations and benefits relating to gold recovered from it.

I think the Treasury Solicitor would be prudent to continue the existing arrangements with yourselves for a number of reasons some of which are as follows:

1. Your continued monitoring of the site and close relationship with local authorities and other groups are an essential safeguard against illicit operations,

2. Your continued work and presence on the site from year to year, not only as owners of the hull but also in effective possession of it, should prevent the accrual of third party rights of salvor in possession which could otherwise operate to exclude any Treasury endorsed initiatives.

3. Being in effective control and possession of the wreck site and being seen to work it also provides yourself with status of salvor in possession as far as cargo is concerned. Even as a mere owner of the hull there are arguments that an action for unjust enrichment can lie where trespass (ie interference) to the hull is occasioned in pursuit of financial gain through recovery of cargo. By "waiving the tort" of trespass and suing under equity the claim moves from compensation for actual damage to your property to a claim on the benefits derived from its use.

4. There is also the practical problem of commerciality and competence. Both Nick and John know the subsea industry very well having been responsible for developing some of the technology now in use. Similarly, I have been recently involved in deep water salvage operations with leading French and American companies. Accordingly, between us we still have a reasonable idea as to the technical and commercial restraints operating on site as well as the operational constraints which have been learned in the course of well over £500,000 worth of operations on the site. A serious operator relying on investment funds would be thinking in terms of 10 X capital risked and although an operator using redundant equipment would require less, personnel and supplies would still be a heavy cost to be capitalised. As you know the

wreck site within short periods can be covered by sand or large boulders, operations can be impeded by local fishermen which can use explosives, buoying of the site, or deployment of heavy equipment difficult. For these reasons one is essentially looking at opportunistic operations for which a local presence is again more than just desirable and saves considerable time in expenditure in planning and local support.

I would hope that bearing these factors in mind the Treasury would prefer to have you working with them under a contractual agreement than to expose themselves to the more fluid ones of third party salvage or worst of all unpublicised illicit operations.

With all the best wishes for success and with thanks for your past help.

Nick Sinclair-Brown

John Clarke

Nick Sills

THE DOCUMENT OF TRANSFER READS AS FOLLOWS:

ERIC COSSUM of 2, Boulogne Court, Folkestone, Kent, ("Mr. Cossum") and

CONSORTIUM RECOVERY LIMITED whose registered office is at Baldwin Barn, Swaffham Prior, Cambridgeshire CB5 OLD ("CR")

WHEREAS

1. By an agreement dated the 21st. April 1969 ("the original agreement") the Ministry of Defence transferred title in the *Laurentic* to Mr. Cossum together with the benefit of an undertaking as to payment by the Bank of England (on behalf of the Treasury) in respect of any gold bullion salved from it.

2. By an agreement of the 6th. June 1979 and 22nd. November 1985 ("the Deeds of Variation") the undertaking as to payment to be made to the Bank of England was varied.

3. By an agreement dated the 22nd. November 1985 ("the transfer agreement") Mr. Cossum transferred his title to the *Laurentic* and CR.

4. Under the same agreement CR assumed the benefit of the payments due under the Deeds of Variation in respect of any bullion salved from it and assumed associated delivery obligations.

5. Despite a number of operations the 20 gold bars referred to in the second recital to the Original Agreement remain unrecovered and prior to its voluntary dissolution CR wishes to withdraw from its interests under the Transfer Agreement, in favour of the resumption by Mr. Cossum of his prior title and interests.

NOW IT IS HEREBY AGREED AS FOLLOWS

1. In consideration of the payment by Mr. Cossum of £1 receipt of which is hereby acknowledged CR hereby transfers to Mr. Cossum its title to the *Laurentic*.

2. Mr. Cossum agrees (subject to concurrence of the Treasury in confirming continuance for the benefit of Mr. Cossum of the existing undertakings to CR as to payment for bullion salved from the *Laurentic*) to resume the liabilities under clause 2 of the original agreement.

3. The invalidity or unenforceability of any provision of this Agreement shall not affect the validity or enforceability of any provision but shall be severed from it so that the balance of the Agreement shall be construed and enforced as if the Agreement did not contain the particular provision held to be invalid or unenforceable.

IN WITNESS WHEREOF

Each party has caused this document to be executed for it in two originals to take effect from 11th. November 1995.

DULY EXECUTED ON BEHALF OF THE COMPANY BY ITS DIRECTORS

Signatures followed.

At the end of Consortium's operation Eric Cossum had become very discouraged. "It's time to give up," he said. "Because of our ages it is too much for us. We know the gold is there but it will have to take a different approach and not use a big salvage boat like Consortium Recovery's because it would cost a great deal of money. We believe it should be done with a boat just big enough to do the work. There is no easy way to recover the gold or the Cossum Syndicate Ltd. would have found it. But we are not big enough to do so and I believe it's time to give up and like Consortium Recovery Ltd said, it needs to be done like they said at the end of their operations which is as follows:

As no individual gold bars were found in a fairly extensive search of "Damant's" gold area there is a greater likely hood of the remaining gold being located in one place. It is possible that two or three boxes have escaped into a corridor or shaft as the ship broke up. The most practical approach for a further attempt may be to consider the feasibility of running a cheaper operation over a longer period. The operation would support its daily cost by recovering scrap from the wreck. (Most of the scrap is off the wreck, because of "Damant's" clearance of all metal above the engine room). In the initial period a great deal of scrap steel, brass and lead could be recovered using a grab. later some cutting, tearing or blasting could release other sections. This could be run on a break even with the possibility of bonus bars of gold.

The gold prices for the 20 remaining gold bars would be worth around £5,000,000."

CHAPTER SEVEN

HOAX GOLD AND THE SECOND LAURENTIC

A few years ago rumours swept Donegal, and it was reported by Mary Garvin on Highland Radio Donegal's most popular radio station, that a bar of gold worth £250,000 had been found by a 12-man strong British diving team who had returned to England. The rumour was investigated by the Department of the Marine and Customs Officers. Later the Department of the Marine was reported to consider that the find was a hoax. However, many people didn't believe it was a hoax, and that a real gold bar had been found. By then the find was being reported on CNN in America. Here is the true tale of the hoax gold.

On a quiet Saturday morning in 1992, Mary Garvin, News reporter for Highland Radio, was relaxing with a cup of tea when the phone rang. The voice on the other end babbled something about a gold bar being found on the wreck of White Star Liner, *Laurentic,* by some divers from Manchester. The Englishman's voice was very unclear and Mary, an astute journalist, asked him to give her the number of the phone box he was ringing from and she would ring back to verify that the caller was genuine. When she rang the number Mary recognised it as the phone number of Rita's Bar in Portsalon. She immediately got through to Dave Marks, the diver who reported that the bar of gold had been found, and did an over-the-phone quick interview with him. Believing the call was genuine and that she had a scoop, Mary quickly reported everything that Dave Marks told her. Within minutes of her broadcast it was picked up by many of the major radio stations. The following week the 'gold find' was all over the newspapers and reported on CNN in America. The hoax was eventually exposed, but not before some very lengthy and intense investigation of Ray and the divers by Customs and Excise and Department of the Marine officials. Five years later, on a television programme called, 'Confessions', the true story came out.

According to Dave Marks, the hoax was suggested by Fergus and Phillip Gribbon, two Belfast brothers who had been diving with the Manchester R.A.D.G. diving club on the *Laurentic.* But it was one of the Manchester divers who had made up a Fools Gold Ingot and, after the dive, they had brought it into Rita's Bar wrapped in newspaper. The imitation bar was made of brass and filled with lead and had a brass bottom braised onto it.

Fergus explained: 'We decided to wind up everyone in the bar that we had found a real gold ingot from the wreck. Everyone was trying to get a good look at it. To heighten the excitement we kept the brass ingot partly covered in paper. But it was Dave Marks who suggested we phone the local radio station. It was Dave who fooled Mary.'

Later when Mary came on the programme she explained it had been tough for her after the hoax but she said it had been a lot tougher for Ray Cossum, who had been thoroughly investigated by Customs and Excise officials. At the end of the programme Ray appeared carrying the bar of fools gold. Ray pretended to be still angry with the divers and at the end of the show he showed the bottom of the bar with the words, 'Fools Gold R.A.D.G.' written on it.

Down through the years there have been many reports of found gold on the Laurentic. All have been untrue. Last year, on 7th. April, these words headed The Irish News.

DIVER FINDS £2M IN SHIP WRECK.

EXCLUSIVE

A Northern Ireland diver has discovered £2million in gold bullion, it was claimed yesterday.

Veteran diver Ray Cossum is set to land the treasure lost from a ship sunk by German mines in January 1917. *(The report went on to tell the story of how the great liner sank).* In the ensuing years more and more of the valuable cargo was raised until 1924, when the final box was located.

Ray Cossum, from Derry, who now owns the salvage rights to the ship - revealed research showed that, as the box was being lifted from the *Laurentic,* a cable snapped throwing it back into the sea and away from the wreck.

"Despite many efforts since then the box has never been recovered," he revealed.

A former Royal Navy diver, Mr. Cossum has always been an avid diver and enthusiastic swimmer. In 1970 he swam the English Channel, while in 1978, with a number of other swimmers from Derry, he broke the world record for a relay swim of the Channel which still stands.

The wreck of the *Laurentic* passed through many hands since 1917 until Mr.

Ray Cossum with the Fools' Gold.

Cossum, his son, Des and his brother Eric, also a diver, gained salvage rights in 1969.

Since then they have dived regularly on the wreck and recovered many artifacts including the heavy guns used to convert the ship into an auxiliary cruiser for war purposes.

The Cossum brothers frequently allowed other diving teams to search the wreck under strict legal agreements, but no sign of the final gold box was ever located until last year.

With the help of a U.S. team of divers using the latest side scan radar equipment, Mr. Cossum now believes he has found the last valuable gold.

"It's lying on the seabed but I'm saying no more than that," the Derry diver said.

Under salvage law, Ray stands to gain quite a lot of money with his brother, although the ownership of the gold still lies with the British Treasury.

"I have no doubt about it. I know it is the box," Mr. Cossum said.

Understandably the veteran diver declined to say when he intended raising the mysterious box other than to confirm that it would be some time this Summer. (ends)

Quite a story isn't it. But the following story of another *Laurentic* is part of the second World War's history.

THE SECOND LAURENTIC.

Otto Kretschmer was one of the greatest U-boat Commanders of the Second World War and it was Herr Kretschmer who sank the second *Laurentic*.

Laurentic 2 was a Cunard White Star Liner built by Harland and Wolff in 1927. She was over 3,000 tonnes heavier than the first *Laurentic* being, 183 metres long and with a beam of 69 metres. She had triple expansion engines with low-pressure turbine triple screws. Like the first *Laurentic, Laurentic 2* was commandeered by the Admiralty when the Second World War broke out.

Otto Kretschmer

In July 1935 *Laurentic 2* crashed into a cruiser called the *Napier Star* off the Skerries in the Irish Sea with the loss of six lives. Badly holed, the *Laurentic* lay for over four years in a scrap yard waiting for orders to break her up. But as the war began the Admiralty needed all the sea-going craft they could get, so the second *Laurentic* a 1,500 passenger cruise liner, joined the Royal Navy on September, 1939, as an armed cruiser, and used to patrol the Western Approaches.

Laurentic II

On that fateful day, after receiving a May day from a ship called the *Casanare*, *Laurentic 2* headed towards a position just off Bloody Foreland, Co. Donegal, to give assistance. Her captain, E. Vivian, knew the danger, and was on the look out for German submarines known to be in the area.

Below, Commander Kretschmer, on the submarine U-99, slowly raised his periscope and saw the sinking *Casanare*. Knowing help would be on the way he waited.

Another ship *was* on the way. It was a former Blue Funnel Liner called the *Patroclus*.

When *Laurentic 2* came on the scene Kretschmer ordered two torpedoes to be fired at her. One hit the bows and the other amidships. Captain Vivian, 50 officers and 320 ratings survived. Then as the *Patroclus* came to their rescue to pick up survivors Kretschmer ordered one torpedo to be fired. It hit the *Patroclus* on the bows yet she stayed afloat. Even after another two torpedoes hit her the *Patroclus* would not sink. The reason for this was because her hold was filled with empty containers, which kept her afloat for over five hours. It took another two torpedoes to sink her. On his way out into the Atlantic Kretschmer sank another cruiser called the *Forfar*. Her Captain G. Wynter, 33 officers and 250 crewmen, were rescued. Survivors from all the cruisers were picked up the following morning by H.M.S. *Achates* and another ship.

Strangely one of the dead from *Laurentic 2*, A.B. Roy Beverley McLeod, D/JX. 181713 R.N., age 34, is buried in grave 11, which is adjacent to the communal grave of the first *Laurentic* dead.

During World War Two Otto Kretschmer sank 44 ships. It is a strange coincidence that he was born the year the White Star Liner and the most famous of them all, *Titanic* sank.

Kretschmer was a fluent English speaker, having learned to speak it in England. His first *success* on becoming a U-boat Commander was sinking the Danish tanker, *Danmark*. Kretschmer was famous for using only one torpedo to destroy a ship. The outstanding time in his career was sinking the three ships, *Laurentic 2, Patroclus* and the *Forfar* - total tonnage 45,000.

Kretschmer was decorated by Adolph Hitler with the equivalent of the Victoria Cross. He was captured by the British in March, 1941, after depth charges dropped by H.M.S. *Walker* damaged his submarine. He spent more than 6six years in British jails.

Years ago Ray wrote to Otto telling him of his intention to get a book published on the *Laurentic* and asking him could he help in finding out more about the submarine that sank the first *Laurentic*. He received this reply.

OTTO KRETSCHMER   14/12/68

Dear Mr. Cossum,

I am sorry I am not able to supply you with the photos of World War One and U-boat 99 of World War Two. But I can forward you the address of a gentleman who has collected photographs of submarines of both World Wars. I am very much interested in your book and would be grateful if you would inform me when it will be issued and what will be its title. I wish you a merry Christmas and a happy new year.

Yours Truly

Otto Kretschmer.

Otto, Germany's U-Boat Ace died on vacation in Bavaria in 1998 after an accident.

So it is quite a coincidence that both Laurentics had been sunk in the two World Wars. Perhaps not a coincidence when you consider it was reported at the time of the building of the first Laurentic that superstitious workers at Harland and Wolff had said that the name Laurentis was unlucky. This is hard to deny when you think of the unfortunate seamen who died on their last voyages.

Finally I would like to say that when I was asked to write about the Laurentic and her historical connections I had my doubts that the 20 missing gold ingots and the safe were still lying amongst the wreckage. I have no doubt now after much research that most of the gold bars and the safe are there. Some day they will be found.

Ray is still diving and is searching for a wreck called the Saldanha which sailed from Derry to fight in the Napoleonic War in December 1811. It was because of this tragedy that the Portsalon lighthouse was built. Ray already has information on the Saldanha's wheareabouts and is pictured here with a cannonade from her. I have no doubt this exceptional man will succeed in finding her.

JACK SCOLTOCK 2000

Cannonade from HMS *Saldanha* wreck which
resulted in the deaths of the whole crew.

ACKNOWLEDGEMENTS:-

VICTOR FOSTER

THE LONDONDERRY SENTINEL

THE DERRY JOURNAL

ANDY RIDGE -
DIVER MAGAZINE

THE IRISH NEWS

DERMOT FRANCIS -
HARBOUR MUSEUM, DERRY.

BREIDGE HENDERSON -
HARBOUR MUSEUM, DERRY

STEPHEN NAYLOR

JOAN HORSLEY,
PLUMSTEAD, LONDON, ENGLAND
PROFESSIONAL RESEARCHER.

GEORGE CATON
(grandson of Peter Caton)

PETE THRELFALL,
MERSEYSIDE, ENGLAND.

JOHN DAVIDSON

DAVID BIGGER

TERRY MCDONALD

PEARSE HENDERSON
(Historian)

JACQUELINE WITHERS -
COMMONWEALTH WAR GRAVES COMMISSION.

THE COMPLETE LIST OF CASUALTIES OF H.M.S. LAURENTIC WW1. FOLLOWS:

FRANCE.
BEAUMONT-HAMEL (NEWFOUNDLAND) MEMORIAL-Somme

AYLES, Seaman, ALEXANDER, 1697X. Newfoundland Royal Naval Reserve. 25th January 1917.
  Age 28. Son of James and Mary Ayles, of Bonavista.
BENOIT, Seaman, JAMES JOHN, 2272X. Newfoundland Royal Naval Reserve. 25th January 1917.
  Age 24. Son of John and Alice Benoit, of Stephenville, St. George.
BRENTON, Seaman, GEORGE, 1502X. Newfoundland Royal Naval Reserve. 25th January 1917.
  Age 23. Son of George and Ellen Brenton, of Port au Bras, Burin.
BRINSTON, Seaman, LESLIE, 305X. Newfoundland Royal Naval Reserve. 25th January 1917.
  Age 32. Son of Robert William and Amelia Brinston; Husband of Susie Brinston, of North Harbour, Placentia Bay.
CUMBY, Seaman, ERASTUS, 1777X. Newfoundland Royal Naval Reserve. 25th January 1917.
  Age 24. Son of George and Hannah Cumby.
FREAKE, Seaman, EPHRAIM, 2213X. Newfoundland Royal Naval Reserve. 25th January 1917.
  Age 21. Son of Mrs. Mary Freake, of Joe Batt's Arm, Fogo.
GOSS, Seaman, ELDRED, 357X Newfoundland Royal Naval Reserve. 25th January 1917.
  Age 30. Husband of Elizabeth Goss of Queen's Cove, Random South, Trinity Bay.
KING, Private, JABEZ WILLIAM, 2718. Royal Newfoundland Regiment. Died on board S.S. Laurentic en route for Newfoundland for discharge. 9th August 1916.
  Age 28. Son of Mathew and Phoebe King, of Lewisporte, Twillingate.
MUGFORD, Seaman, JACOB, 531X Newfoundland Royal Naval Reserve. 25th January 1917.
  Age 31. Son of William and Lavinia Mugford; Husband of Ethel May Wood (formerly Mugford), of Leopold Post Office, P.Q. Canada.
MURPHY, Seaman, LAWRENCE, 1817X Newfoundland Royal Naval Reserve. 25th January 1917.
  Age 22. Only son of James and Sarah Murphy, of Conception Harbour.
MURRAY, Seaman, JAMES, 1446X. Royal Naval Reserve. 25th January 1917.
  Age 21. Son of John and Margaret Murray.
PUDDICOMBE, Seaman, WILLIAM, 2136X. Newfoundland Royal Naval Reserve. 25th January 1917.
  Age 28. Son of Frederick and Annie Puddicombe.
RANDALL, Seaman. FREDERICK, 816X. Newfoundland Royal Naval Reserve. 25th January 1917.
  Age 26. Son of John and Elizabeth Randall, of Fogo.
ROGERS, Seaman, SIMEON, 1138X. Newfoundland Royal Naval Reserve. 25th January 1917.
  Age 32. Son of Willis and Sarah Rogers; Husband of Bertha Rogers, of 176, Water Street, St. John's.
SMITH, Seaman, LUKE, 979X. Newfoundland Royal Naval Reserve. 25th January 1917.
  Age 30. Husband of Isabella Smith, of Butler Cove, Random South, Trinity Bay.
TUCKER, Seaman, JOHN CHARLES, 895X. Newfoundland Royal Naval Reserve. 25th January 1917.
  Age 31. Son of John George and Sarah Fanny Tucker; Husband of Mary Ann Tucker, of Ship Cove, Port de Grave.
YETMAN, Seaman, CLEMENT, 1458X. Newfoundland Royal Naval Reserve. 25th January 1917.
  Age 25. Son of Moses and Selina Yetman, of Harbour Grace South.
YOUNG, Seaman, WALLACE, 1884X. Newfoundland Royal Naval Reserve. 25th January 1917.
  Age 21. Son of Mrs. Ellen Young, of Flat Bay, St. George.

HONG KONG.
HONG KONG CEMETERY-

FORSTER, Private, J.E. 10890 (CH) Royal Marine Light Infantry. 27th June 1916. Husband of Annie Forster, of 65, Princess St, Llanelly, Carmarthenshire. Born in London. 168. 8154.

IRELAND. REPUBLIC of
ARKLOW CEMETERY- COUNTY WICKLOW.

KENNY, Seaman, JOHN, 4996A. Royal Naval Reserve. 25th January 1917.
    Age 22. Son of James Kenny, of 32, Fair Green, Arklow, South. 3NN. 12 East.

COCKHILL CATHOLIC CEMETERY-COUNTY DONEGAL

CRAIG, Steward, THOMAS HUGH, 751343. Mercantile Marine Reserve. 25th January 1917.
    Age 32. Son of John and Jane Craig; Husband of Lily Craig, of Bangor Arms Hotel, Killough,
    Co. Down. In South part.
MORGAN, Lieutenant, RICHARD. Royal Naval Reserve. 25th January 1917. In South part.

UPPER FAHAN CHURCH OF IRELAND CHURCHYARD-COUNTY DONEGAL

ABBOTT, Private, JOHN ARTHUR, CH/11488. Royal Marine Light Infantry. 25th January 1917.
    Age 35. Son of Alexander and Jane E. Abbott. Born at Cambridge. Previously served 12 years in R.M.L.I.;
    Rejoined in 1914.
ARCHER, Greaser, GEORGE WALTER, 440715. Mercantile Marine Reserve. 25th January 1917.
ASTBURY, Corporal, HERBERT THOMAS, PLY/8778. Royal Marine Light Infantry. 25th January 1917.
    Age 36. Son of Joseph Astbury; Husband of Florence Astbury, of 13, East St., Stonehouse, Plymouth.
AUSTIN, Chief Armourer, RUFUS SAMUEL MARDON, 155807. Royal Marines. 25th January 1917.
BAKER, Private, WILLIAM, ALFRED, CH/18143. Royal Marine Light Infantry. 25th January 1917.
BYERS, Greaser, GEORGE, 903348. Mercantile Marine Reserve. 25th January 1917.
CAMPBELL, Trimmer, CHARLES, 852424. Mercantile Marine Reserve. 25th January 1917.
CARLISLE, Engineer Lieutenant, JAMES. Royal Naval Reserve. 25th January 1917.
    Age 43. Son of the late Rear-Admiral (Engineer) James Carlisle, R.N.; Husband of the late Florence Edith
    Clegg.
CATLIN, Private, ALBERT FRANCIS, CH/17516. Royal Marine Light Infantry. 25th January 1917.
    Age 22. Son of Mr. and Mrs. Alfred Francis Catlin, of 211, Horninglow Rd., Burton-on-Trent.
CATON, Engineer Sub-Lieutenant, PETER. Royal Naval Reserve. 25th January 1917.
    Age 41. Son of the late Peter and Jane Caton, of Birkenhead; Husband of Emily Caton, of 35, Briardale Rd.,
    Birkenhead.
CHAPMEN, Steward, JOSEPH, 737038. Mercantile Marine Reserve. 25th January 1917.
    Age 21. Son of Joseph and Harriett Chapmen.
COAFFEE, Master at Arms, GEORGE EDWIN, 182942 (Dev.) Royal Navy. 25th January 1917.
    Age 39. Husband of Edith J. Coaffee, of Greatlands Place, Swilly, Plymouth. Served in the South African War.
    Royal Human Society's Medal.
COLLACOTT, Petty Officer Ist. Class. THOMAS JAMES, 142707 (Dev.) Royal Navy. 25th January 1917.
COVE, Chief Writer, AWDRY LAURENCE, 874979. Mercantile Marine Reserve. 25th January 1917.
    Age 19. Son of Philip Chadder Cove and Edith Cove, of Crossways, Herbert Rd., Salcombe, Devon.
COYLE, Fireman, JOHN, 369480. Mercantile Marine Reserve. 25th January 1917.
    Age 34. Son of John and Mary Coyle; Husband of Cathcrine Coyle, of 14, Poulter Rd., Aintree, Liverpool.
CRAZE, Fireman, THOMAS, 809365. Mercantile Marine Reserve. 25th January 1917.
CUNNINGHAM, Private, WILLIAM, PLY/18574. Royal Marine Light Infantry. 25th January 1917.
DAYMOND, Engineer Lieutenant, GEORGE HENRY. Royal Naval Reserve. 25th January 1917.
EDNEY, Petty Officer Ist. Class, JAMES HIGHFIELD, 113286 (Dev.) Royal Navy. 25th January 1917.
    Age 52. Son of Henry Edney, of Amble, Northumberland; Husband of Henrietta Edney, of Highfield, Four
    Marks, Alton, Hants.
EDWARDS, Painter, FREDERICK. Mercantile Marine Reserve. 25th January 1917.
FISHER, Electrical Engineer, RICHARD. Mercantile Marine Reserve. 25th January 1917.
FLEMING, Seaman, John, 2320A (Dev.) Royal Naval Reserve. 25th January 1917.
    Age 25. Son of John Fleming, of Lower Dunmore East, Co. Waterford.
FORSHAW, Fireman, JOHN, 681580. Mercantile Marine Reserve. 25th January 1917.
GAMBLE, Leading Seaman, ALBERT EDWARD, 194663 (Dev.) Royal Navy. 25th January 1917.
GIBBINS, Engineer Lieutenant, JAMES WILLIAM, Royal Naval Reserve. 25th January 1917.
GILL, Petty Officer Ist Class. GEORGE, 195552 (Po.) Royal Navy. 25th January 1917.
GRAY, Engine Room Artificer 4th Class, FREDERICK BALFOUR, 4/1823. Royal Navy Volunteer Reserve.
    25th January 1917.

HALLIDAY, Shipwright, REES. Mercantile Marine Reserve. 25th January 1917.
> Age 25. Son of Thomas and Rachel Halliday, of Jarrow-on-Tyne.

HARGATE, Private, LEONARD CH/18352. Royal Marine Light Infantry. 25th January 1917.

HEANEY, Seaman, JOHN, 4997A (Dev.) Royal Naval Reserve. 25th January 1917.

HILL, Seaman, ROBERT HARRAD, 2107C. Royal Naval Reserve. 25th January 1917.
> Age 37. Husband of Florence Glanville (formerly Hill), of 18, Looe St., Plymouth.

HINDS, Trimmer, ALEC, 787272. Mercantile Marine Reserve. 25th January 1917.

HODGES, Fireman, ARTHUR CHARLES. Mercantile Marine Reserve. 25th January 1917.
> Age 37. Husband of Sarah Hodges, of 38, Wightman St., Custom House, London.

HONEY, Signalman, SAMUEL STUART, Bristol Z/1664. Royal Naval Volunteer Reserve. 25th January 1917.
> Age 19. Son of John Henry and Fanny Honey, of Chapel Ground, West Looe, Cornwall.

HOOPER, Seaman, SAMUEL MAYO, 18658. Newfoundland Royal Naval Reserve. 25th January 1917.
> Age 20. Son of James and Frances J. Hooper, of Crestin, Mortier bay, Newfoundland.

HYDE, Private, GEORGE ERNEST, PLY/15426. Royal Marine Light Infantry. 25th January 1917.
> Age 21. Son of Samuel Ernest and Matilda Hyde, of 43, Gt. Western St., Manchester. Born at Bristol.

JORDAIN, Seaman, SAMUEL, 2296C. Royal Naval Reserve. 25th January 1917. Husband of Ethel Jordain, of 5, Higher Terrace, Brixham, Devon.

LAVERTY, Shipwright 2nd Class, AMBROSE, M/21469(Dev.) Royal Navy. 25th January 1917.
> Age 29. Son of Ambose and Hannah Laverty, of Hebburn-on-Tyne; Husband of Violet Hunt (formerly Laverty), of 169, Frances Avenue, Southsea.

LYNCH, Seaman, MICHAEL, 5860A(Dev.) Royal Naval Reserve. 25th January 1917.
> Age 28. Son of Mr. R. Lynch, of Buckley's Lane, Youghal, Co. Cork.

MILLER, Seaman, DAVID, 3659A(Dev.) Royal Naval Reserve. 25th January 1917.

MOORHOUSE, Butcher, EDWARD, 640251. Mercantile Marine Reserve. 25th January 1917.

NORISH, Chief Petty Officer, ALFRED, 136926(Dev.) Royal Navy. 25th January 1917.

O'DONNELL, Seaman, COLMAN, 5054A. Royal Naval Reserve. 25th January 1917.
> Age 25. Son of Mr. P. O'Donnell, of Long Walk, Galway.

REYNOLDS, Acting Bombardier, MONTAGUE JAMES, RMA/10853. Royal Marine Artillery. 25th January 1917.

RICHARDSON, Leading Seaman, ARTHUR, 2864A. Royal Naval Reserve. 25th January 1917.

ROBERTS, Plumber, JOSEPH. Mercantile Marine Reserve. 25th January 1917.
> Age 25. Son of Joseph and Annie Roberts, of 10, Sidney Rd., Bootle.

ROYLE, Sailmaker, FRANCIS LEONARD, 735086. Mercantile Marine Reserve. 25th January 1917.
> Age 25. Son of Francis and Elizabeth Ann Royle, of Essendon, Victoria, Australia.

RUSHTON, Steward, CHARLES HENRY, 643229. Mercantile Marine Reserve. 25th January 1917.

SHEEDY, Able Seaman, FREDERICK ALLEN, 2426. H.M.A.S. "Sydney" (H.M.S. Laurentic) Royal Australian Navy. Killed in loss of H.M.S. "Laurentic" by mine explosion off N. Irish Coast, 25th January 1917.
> Age 19. Son of James and Annie J. Sheedy, of Ocean View Hospital, Solomon St., Freemantle, Western Australia. Born at Adamstown, New South Wales.

SKINNER, Fireman, HUGH. Mercantile Marine Reserve. 25th January 1917.
> Age 25. Son of Alexander and Annie Skinner, of 6, Back St., Hilton, Fearn, Ross-shire.

SMITH, Private, JOHN ROBERT, 120393. Royal Marine Light Infantry. 25th January 1917.

SNELGROVE, Private, FREDERICK JAMES, CH/20447. Royal Marine Light Infantry. 25th January 1917.

SUTTON, Private, ALFRED, CH/18110. Royal Marine Light Infantry. 25th January 1917.

TARDIVEL, Petty Officer Stoker, FRANK, 279894 (Po.) Royal Navy. 25th January 1917.

TAYLOR, Chief Petty Officer, ALBERT EDWARD, 156355. Royal Navy. 25th January 1917.

THOMPSON, Trimmer, JOHN, 885539. Mercantile Marine Reserve. 25th January 1917.
> Age 17. Son of James and Jane Thompson, of 38, Rydal St., Everton, Liverpool. Born at Banks, Southport, Lancs.

TODMAN, Trimmer, ALFRED, 816995. Mercantile Marine Reserve. 25th January 1917.

WALLACE, Steward, CHARLES JAMES. Mercantile Marine Reserve. 25th January 1917.
> Age 41. Son of the late Charles James and Jane Wallace, of Birkenhead.

WHITE, Seaman, ARTHUR, 1447X Newfoundland Royal Naval Reserve. 25th January 1917.
> Age 27. Son of George and Nellie White, of Shalop Cove, St. George's, Newfoundland.

WINDIBANK, Able Seaman, PERCY HENRY, 232300. Royal Navy. 25th January 1917.
> Age 28. Son of John and Mary Windibank, of Cranleigh, Surrey.

WOODROW, Able Seaman, WILLIAM FULTON, Clyde 3/1882. Royal Naval Volunteer Reserve. 25th January 1917.
> Age 23. Only son of Mr. James P. Woodrow of 31, Dover Street, Glasgow.

YULE, Signalman, VICTOR, Clyde Z/7978. Royal Naval Volunteer Reserve. 25th January 1917.
    Age 19. Son of George and Bathea Yule, of 13, Blackness Avenue, Dundee.

SOUTH AFRICA
CAPETOWN (MAITLAND) CEMETERY-WESTERN CAPE

MELANEY, Chief Steward, A. Mercantile Marine Reserve. 22nd. September 1916. Sec. 4. 95868A. Sp.Mem.

UNITED KINGDOM
CHATHAM NAVAL MEMORIAL-KENT

ABBOTT, Deck Hand, MAXWELL, 10521 D. A. Royal Marine Reserve. Killed by mine explosion off Irish
    Coast 25th January 1917.
    Age 20. Son of Roger H. and Janet Abbott, of Bonavista Newfoundland, 26.

BIRKENHEAD, Seaman, THOMAS ARCHIBALD, 2616A. Royal naval reserve. Killed by mine explosion off Irish
    Coast 25th January 1917. 26.

BOWER, Private, ALWYNE, CH/17305. Royal Marine Light Infantry. Killed by mine explosion off Irish Coast 25th
    January 1917.

BULLER, Wireless Telegraph Operator, SYDNEY JOSEPH, 414WTC. Royal Naval Reserve. Killed by mine
    explosion off Irish Coast 25th January 1917.
    Age 23. Son of Arthur and Edna Eliza Buller, of 49, Randall St., Maidstone, Kent. 25.

CARR, Stoker, EDWARD, 3955/S. Royal Naval Reserve. Killed by mine explosion off Irish Coast 25th January
    1917.
    Age 29. Son of John and Margaret Carr, of 54, Dock St., Tyne Dock, South Shields. 27.

CARTER, Private, NORMAN, CH/20284. Royal Light Infantry. Killed by mine explosion off Irish Coast 25th
    January 1917.
    Age 18. Son of Lewis and Eliza Carter, of Slant Gate, Kirkburton, Huddersfield. 25.

COCHRAN, Private, JOHN, CH/19804. Royal Marine Light Infantry. Killed by mine explosion off Irish Coast 25th
    January 1917.
    Age 20. Son of Robert and Margaret Cochran, of 1974, Maryhill Rd., Glasgow. 25.

CULL, Private, JOSEPH WILLET, CH/20242. Royal Marine Light Infantry. Killed by mine explosion off Irish Coast
    25th January 1917.
    Age 18. Son of Charles and Ellen Cull, of Wallasey, Cheshire. 25.

DAVIES, Ordinary Signalman, JOHN VICTOR, Tyneside 1/158. Royal Naval Volunteer Reserve. killed by mine
    explosion off Irish Coast 25th January 1917.
    Age 25. Son of Thomas and Harriett Davies, of 105, West View, Gluehouse Lane, Newcastle-on-Tyne. 27.

DE BLAQUIERE, Sub-Lieutenant, ALLAN BOYLE, H.M.S. "Antrim." (H.M.S. "Laurentic"). Royal Navy.
    Killed by mine explosion off Irish Coast 25th January 1917.
    Age 21. Son of William, 6th Baron de Blaquiere of Ardkill, and Lucienne, Daughter of G.E. Desbarats, of
    Montreal, Canada. Served at the action off Heligoland. 20.

FISHER, Private, CHARLES ALBERT, CH/18880. Royal Marine Light Infantry. Killed by mine explosion off Irish
    Coast 25th January 1917.
    Age 19. Son of John H. and Annie Fisher, of 12, Delverton Rd., Walsworth, London. 25.

GENTLE, Private, JOHN CH/18345. Royal Marine Light Infantry. Killed by mine explosion off Irish Coast 25th
    January 1917.
    Age 22. Son of Mrs. Fanny Henning (formerly Gentle), of 6, Church Path Cottages, Woodside Lane,
    North Finchley, London. 25.

GOODALL, Private, GEORGE, CH/18168. Royal Marine Light Infantry. Killed by mine explosion off Irish
    Coast 25th January 1917.
    Age 20. Son of Pollie Maria Goodall, of 96, Station Rd., Beeston, Notts. 25.

GOODALL, Signalman, WILFRED HENRY, LondonZ/5087. Royal Naval Volunteer Reserve. Killed by mine
    explosion off Irish Coast 25th January 1917.
    Age 22. Only son of Emily Goodall, of 41, Burlington Rd., Colchester, Essex; and the late W. Goodall. 27.

HANCOCK, Private, JOSEPH, CH/17678.Royal Marine Light Infantry. Killed by mine explosion off Irish Coast
    25th January 1917.
    Age 24. Son of the late Thomas and Louisa Hancock. 25.

HAWKES, Private, EDWARD JAMES, CH/20165. Royal Marine Light Infantry. Killed by mine explosion off Irish
    Coast 25th January 1917.
    Age 18. Son of Edward and Annie Hawkes, of 19, Milbourne Rd., Hanworth, Middx. 25.

HITCHEN, Private, FRANK, CH/20234. Royal Marine Light Infantry. Killed by mine explosion off Irish Coast 25th January 1917.
> Age 18. Son of Frank and Eliza Hitchen, of 2, Pleasant View, Blackwood, Stacksteads, Bacup, Lancs. 25.

LESTER, Lance Corporal, JOSEPH RICHARD, CH/13181. Royal Marine Light Infantry. Killed by mine explosion off Irish Coast 25th January 1917.
> Age 28. Son of Emily Lester, of 65, Skinner St., Chatham, and the late Joseph Lester. 25.

MacAULAY, Seaman, AULAY, 3360A. Royal Naval Reserve. Killed by mine explosion off Irish Coast 25th January 1917.
> Age 29. Son of Aulay and Catherine MacAulay (nee MacLean), of 15, Breaselet, Stornoway, Ross-shire. 26.

MACDONALD, Seaman, ANGUS, 3467A. Royal Naval Reserve. Killed by mine explosion off Irish Coast 25th January 1917.
> Age 25. Son of Norman and Mary Macdonald, of 7, Tobson, Bernera, Stornoway, Ross-shire. 26.

MACDONALD, Seaman, NORMAN, 3279B. Royal Naval Reserve. Killed By mine explosion off Irish Coast 25th January 1917. Son of Norman and Christy Macdonald, of 5, Breaclet, Bernera, Stornoway, Ross-shire. 26.

MARSHALL, Private, WILLIAM JOHN, CH/6175. Royal Marine Light Infantry. Died of heart failure 7th September 1916. 18.

MICKLEBURGH, Private, SIDNEY ARTHUR, CH/17998. Royal Marine Light Infantry. Killed by mine explosion off Irish Coast 25th January 1917.
> Age 20. Son of Harry and Emma Mickleburgh, of 689, Harrow Rd., Willesden, London. 25.

MILLER, Private, ANDREW, CH/17680. Royal Marine Light Infantry. Killed by mine explosion off Irish Coast 25th January 1917.
> Age 21. Son of Mrs. Annie Hogarth, of 29, Highbuckholmside, Galashiels. 25.

NICHOLSON, Seaman, DUNCAN, 5305A. Royal Naval Reserve. Killed by mine explosion off Irish Coast 25th January 1917.
> Age 22. Son of Mr. and Mrs. Malcolm Nicholson, of 22, Gravis, Lochs, Stornoway, Ross-shire. Was present at Antwerp, 1914. 26.

ODELL, Able Seaman, WILLIAM MATTHEW, J/28287. Royal Navy. Killed by mine explosion off Irish Coast 25th January 1917.
> Age 19. Son of Albert and Rachel Feetham Odell, of 55, Hythe St., Dartford, Kent. 22.

PENNEY, Private, EDWARD JAMES, CH/20445. Royal Marine Light Infantry. Killed by mine explosion off Irish Coast 25th January 1917. Son of E.G. and Lucy Penney, of I, Hadley St., Kentish Town, London. 25.

STUBBINGS, Private, GEORGE, CH/20271. Royal Marine Light Infantry. Killed by mine explosion off Irish Coast 25th January 1917.
> Age 18. Son of Annie Stubbings, of Weston, Colville, Cambs. 25.

THEAKSTONE, Able Seaman, JAMES, J/17048. Royal Navy. Killed by mine explosion off Irish Coast 25th January 1917.
> Age 20. Son of Edward and Emily Theakstone, of Bradlow, Ledbury, Herefordshire. Native of St. Pancras, London. 22.

WALTERS, Deck Hand, LESLIE ERNEST, 10382DA. Royal Naval Reserve. Killed by mine explosion off Irish Coast 25th January 1917.
> Age 20. Son of George S. and Mary Ann Walters, of Lamaline, Burin District, Newfoundland. 26.

WENT, Private, FREDERICK ARTHUR MOAT, CH/18255. Royal Marine Light Infantry. Killed by mine explosion off Irish Coast 25th January 1917.
> Age 20. Son of Frederick and Eliza Went (stepmother), of 13, Artillery Rd., Ramsgate, Kent. 25.

WISDOM, Able Seaman, ALBERT JOHN, London Z/2197. Royal Naval Volunteer Reserve. Killed by mine explosion off Irish Coast 25th January 1917.
> Age 19. Son of Solomon and Elizabeth Wisdom, of Acacia Villas, Willington Rd., Maidstone, Kent. 27.

WOODS, Seaman, JOHN ALBERT, 2737A. Royal Naval Reserve. Killed by mine explosion off Irish Coast 25th January 1917.
> Age 30. Son of John and Elizabeth Woods, of Grimsby, Lincs. 26.

WRENCH, Leading Seaman, HERBERT, 198082. (RFR/CH/B/6870). Royal Navy. Killed by mine explosion off Irish Coast 25th January 1917. 21.

YARNTON, Private, EDWIN JAMES, CH/18342. Royal Marine Light Infantry. Killed by mine explosion off Irish Coast 25th January 1917. 25.

CHORLEY (ST. PETER) CHURCHYARD-LANCASHIRE

WORSFOLD, Corporal, WILLIAM, RMA/13209. Royal Marine Artillery. Killed in action by enemy torpedo 25th January 1917.
Age 21. Son of Francis Henry and Emily Louisa Worsfold, of 18, Garfield Terrace, Chorley. 715.

HEISKER ISLAND GRAVES-INVERNESSHIRE

MCNEILL, Lieutenant, W A. Royal Naval Reserve. 25th January 1917.

HOLLYWOOD CEMETERY-COUNTY DOWN

MITCHELL, Engineer Lieutenant, RR,. Royal Naval Reserve. 25th January 1917.
Age 32. Son of Mrs. Jane Mitchell, of 3, Church Avenue, Hollywood. 574.

LIVERPOOL (WEST DERBY) CEMETERY-LANCASHIRE

HAGEN, Serjeant, W. PLY/3160. (RMR/A/619) Royal Marine Light Infantry. 25th January 1917.
Age 49. Son of Michael Hagen, of Liverpool; Husband of Henrietta Maud Hagen, of 59, New Rd., Linbrook, Liverpool. I. C E. 1309.

PLYMOUTH NAVAL MEMORIAL-DEVON

ABBOTT, Seaman, FREDERICK JOHN, 5317B. Royal Naval Reserve. Killed by mine explosion off Irish Coast 25th January 1917.
Age 27. Son of Henry Octavius Abbott and Nelly Abbott, of 2, Seafield Avenue, Great Crosby, Liverpool. 23.

ALLEN, Fireman, WILLIAM, 897504. Mercantile Marine Reserve. Killed by mine explosion off Irish Coast 25th January 1917.
Age 22. Son of William and Mary Allen, of 60, Gt. Georges St., Liverpool. 25.

ANDREWS, Petty Officer 2nd Class, ALBERT HENRY, 160634. Royal Navy. Killed by mine explosion off Irish Coast 25th January 1917.
Age 42. Son of the late George and Jane Andrews, of Buckover, Falfield, Glos. 20.

ANSTIS, Petty Officer 2nd Class, GEORGE HENRY, 143466. Royal Navy. Killed by mine explosion off Irish Coast 25th January 1917.
Age 43. (RFR/DEV/A/3657). Son of the late William Richard Anstis (pensioner, R.N.) husband of Catherine A. Anstis, of 175, Belmont St., New Bridge Rd., Hull. 20.

ASHCROFT, Fireman, ROBERT, 862993. Mercantile Marine Reserve. Killed by mine explosion off Irish Coast 25th January 1917.

ATKINSON, Private, ALFRED WILLIAM, PLY/18693. Royal Marine Light Infantry. Killed by mine explosion off Irish Coast 25th January 1917.
Age 19. Son of Nellie Atkinson, of 55, Lincoln St., Leeholme, Coundon, Co. Durham and the late Frederick Atkinson. 23.

BALDWIN, Steward, WILLIAM EDWARD, 676700. Mercantile Marine Reserve. Killed by mine explosion off Irish Coast 25th January 1917.
Age 23. Husband of Edith Baldwin, of 48, Morecambe St., Anfield, Liverpool. Native of Leicester. 26.

BALL, Storekeeper Ist Class, ERNEST FREDERICK, H.M. Dockyard, Devonport. Royal Navy. Killed by mine explosion off Irish Coast 25th January 1917.
Age 28. Son of Frederick William and Annie Ball, of Plymouth. 26.

BARTLETT, Petty Officer Ist Class, CHARLES, 157842. Royal Navy. Killed by mine explosion off Irish Coast 25th January 1917.
Age 42. (RFR/DEV/B/957) Son of Elizabeth Bartlett, of Birmingham, Husband of Alice Bartlett, of 48, Ada Rd., Smethwick, Staffs. 20.

BEAUMONT, Assistant Paymaster, FREUND. Royal Naval Reserve. Killed by mine explosion off Irish Coast 25th January 1917.
Age 30. Son of William Beaumont, of 344, Strone Rd., Manor Park, London. 23.

BEESLEY, Steward, THOMAS, 597155. Royal Naval Reserve. Killed by mine explosion off Irish Coast 25th January 1917.
Age 42. Son of John and Jane Beesley, of Liverpool; husband of Sarah Beesley, of 10, Warbeck Rd., Orrell Park, Aintree, Liverpool. 26.

BELL, Sub-Lieutenant, LAURENCE WELLINGTON. Royal Marine Reserve. Killed by mine explosion off Irish Coast 25th January 1917. 23.

BELL, Greaser, WILLIAM, 867678. Mercantile Marine Reserve. Killed by mine explosion off Irish Coast 25th January 1917.
Age 35. Son of Mr. and Mrs. James Bell, of 30, Curror St., Selkirk. Native of Alva, Clackmannanshire. 25.

BOWDLER, Fireman, WILLIAM FREDERICK. Mercantile Marine Reserve. Killed by mine explosion off Irish Coast 25th January 1917.
Age 58. Son of Thomas and Elizabeth Bowdler, of Liverpool; husband of Mary Catherine Bowdler, of 27, St. Chrysostom St., Queen's Rd., Liverpool. 25.

BOWER, Blacksmith's Mate, EDWARD, 889166. Mercantile Marine reserve. Killed by mine explosion off Irish Coast 25th January 1917.
Age 41. Son of Ambrose Nicholas Bower and Anna Bower, of 113, Church Rd., Upper Norwood, London. 25.

BRAMHALL, Fireman, THOMAS, 793374. Mercantile Marine Reserve. Killed by mine explosion off Irish Coast 25th January 1917.
Age 23. Son of Jeffrey and Margaret Bramhall, of Liverpool. 25.

BRENNAN, Seaman, PATRICK, 5825A. Royal Naval Reserve. Killed by mine explosion off Irish Coast 25th January 1917.
Age 20. Son of Michael and Mary Brennan, of The Mall, Youghal, Co. Cork. 23.

BROOKS, Scullion, ARTHUR ERNEST, 113434. Mercantile Marine Reserve. Killed by mine explosion off Irish Coast 25th January 1917.
Age 17. Son of Rosina E. Harvey (formerly Brooks), of 18, Doon St., Kirkdale, Liverpool, and the late Ernest Brooks. 26.

BROWN, Engineer Sub-Lieutenant, JAMES ROBERT. Royal Naval Reserve. Killed by mine explosion off Irish Coast 25th January 1917.
Age 33. Son of Samuel Muir Brown; husband of Mary E. Brown, of 63, Kingfield Rd., Orrell Park, Aintree, Liverpool. 23.

BROWNE, Lieutenant, GEORGE EDMUND RANGECROFT. Royal Naval Reserve. Killed by mine explosion off Irish Coast 25th January 1917. 23.

BUCKLEY, Seaman, JOHN, 5077A. Royal Naval Reserve. Killed by mine explosion off Irish Coast 25th January 1917.
Age 21. Son of Patrick and Mary Buckley, of The Mall, Youghal, Co. Cork. 23.

BULLEY, Seaman, THOMAS, 4482B. Royal Naval Reserve. Killed by mine explosion off Irish Coast 25th January 1917.

BURKE, Yeoman of Signals, JOHN. Mentioned in Dispatches, 138847. (RFR/DEV/A/3185) Royal Navy. Killed by mine explosion off Irish Coast 25th January 1917.
Age 45. Son of David and Bridget Burke, of Whitegate, Co. Cork. 21.

BURNS, Seaman, JAMES, 3636B. Royal Naval Reserve. Killed by mine explosion off Irish Coast 25th January 1917.
Age 33. Son of Alexandra and Mary Burns, of Argyllshire; husband of Ellen Burns, of 16, Miranda Rd., Kirkdale, Liverpool. 23.

CAIN, Steward, WILLIAM LEIGH, 681873. Mercantile Marine Reserve. Killed by mine explosion off Irish Coast 25th January 1917.
Age 33. Son of Fanny Cain, of 50, Longland Rd., Wallasey, Cheshire, and the late Phillip Cain. native of Liverpool. 26.

CAMILLERI, Fireman, LAURENCE, 708955. Mercantile Marine Reserve. Killed by mine explosion off Irish Coast 25th January 1917. 25.

CARR, Greaser, JAMES JOSEPH. Mercantile Marine Reserve. Killed by mine explosion off Irish Coast 25th January 1917.
Age 36. Husband of Theresa Carr, of 6, Norfolk St., St. James St., Liverpool. 25.

CHATTERTON, Trimmer, HENRY, 867057. Mercantile Marine Reserve. Killed by mine explosion off Irish Coast 25th January 1917.
Age 20. Son of William James and Leonora Chatterton, of 11, Hankin St., Liverpool. 25.

CHETHAM, Fireman, JAMES. Mercantile Marine Reserve. Killed by mine explosion off Irish Coast 25th January 1917. 25.

CHRISTIAN, Seaman, JOHN, 5148B. Royal Naval Reserve. Killed by mine explosion off Irish Coast 25th January 1917. 23.

CLARK, Assistant Steward. Mercantile Marine Reserve. Killed by mine explosion off Irish Coast 25th January 1917. 26.

COLES, Able Seaman, WILLIAM, J/9294. Royal Navy. Killed by mine explosion off Irish Coast 25th January 1917.
Age 24. Son of William and Mary Jane Coles, of 7, Comton St., Avondale Rd., Redfield, Bristol. 21.

COUGHLAN, Seaman, DENIS, 5113A. Royal Naval Reserve. Killed by mine explosion off Irish Coast 25th January 1917.
Age 21. Son of Nora Coughlan, of Lispatrick Lower, Old Head, Kinsale, Co. Cork. 23.

CRELLIN, Seaman, SAMUEL, 4874B. Royal Naval Reserve. Killed by mine explosion off Irish Coast 25th January 1917.
Age 29. Son of the late William Henry Crellin, of Ramsey, Isle of Man; husband of Jane Crellin, of 16, Harrogate St., Everton, Liverpool. (Five members of the family fell in the Great War.) 23.

CROTTY, Fireman, THOMAS JOHN, 747502. Mercantile Marine Reserve. Killed by mine explosion off Irish Coast 25th January 1917. 25.

CUTHBERT, Petty Officer Ist Class, RALPH, 176117. Royal Navy. Killed by mine explosion off Irish Coast 25th January 1917.
Age 38. Son of Joseph Cuthbert, of Northampton; husband of Edith Maud Cuthbert, of 9, Wake St., Pennycomequick, Plymouth. 20.

DAVIES, Seaman, JOSEPH, 4590A. Royal Naval Reserve. Killed by mine explosion off Irish Coast 25th January 1917. 23.

DINAN, Able Seaman, FRANCIS FREDERICK, Wales Z/2529. Royal Naval Volunteer Reserve. Killed by mine explosion off the Irish Coast 25th January 1917.
Age 24. Son of F. A. and M. C. Dinan, of 28, Gwydr Crescent, Swansea. 24.

DODD, Steward, RICHARD FIRMAN, 692032. Mercantile Marine Reserve. Killed by mine explosion off Irish Coast 25th January 1917.
Age 39. Son of George and Charlotte Dodd, of Richmond, London. 26.

DODDEMEADE, Seaman, FRANK ALEXANDER, 4646B. Royal Naval Reserve. Killed by mine explosion off Irish Coast 25th January 1917.
Age 34. Son of Sydney Doddemeade, of "Thistledown," Coppice Avenue, Shelford, Cambridge; husband of Joanna A. Doddemeade, of 7, Keats St., Bootle, Liverpool. 23.

DONOGHUE, Fireman, John, 908148. Mercantile Marine Reserve. Killed by mine explosion off Irish Coast 25th January 1917.
Age 35. Son of John and Ellen Donoghue; brother of Daniel Donoghue, of Gurteens, Kilganan, Co. Kerry. 25.

DONOVAN, Leading Seaman, JOHN, 219332. (RFR/DEV/B/5996) Royal Navy. Killed by mine explosion off Irish Coast 25th January 1917.
Age 35. Son of James and Kate Donovan (nee Hayes), of Reenogreena, Glandore, Co. Cork. 20.

DOODSON, Cook, ALFRED JAMES. Mercantile Marine Reserve. Killed by mine explosion off Irish Coast 25th January 1917. 26.

DOOLEY, Greaser, PATRICK. Mercantile Marine Reserve. Killed by mine explosion off Irish Coast 25th January 1917.
Age 58. Husband of Alice Mary Dooley; father of Beatrice Massey, of 24, Claughton Rd., Plaistow, London. 25.

DOUGHERTY, Seaman, ALFRED, 3615C. Royal Naval Reserve. Killed by mine explosion off Irish Coast 25th January 1917.
Age 33. Husband of Esther Eleonor Dougherty, of 24, Big Well St., Douglas, Isle of Man. 23.

DOYLE, Seaman, CHRISTOPHER, 5878A. Royal Naval Reserve. Killed by mine explosion off Irish Coast 25th January 1917.
Age 22. Son of Michael and Catherine Doyle, of 220, Commercial Rd., Kirkdale, Liverpool. 23.

DOYLE, Seaman, JOHN, 5367B. Royal Naval Reserve. Killed by mine explosion off Irish Coast 25th January 1917.
Age 36. Son of Annie Doyle, of Ballyhealy, Kilmore, Co. Wexford. Native of Rathaspick, Co. Wexford. 23.

DUSTAN, Boy. JOHN. Mercantile Marine Reserve. Killed by mine explosion off Irish Coast 25th January 1917.
Age 19. Cook's son of James Dustan, of 262, Union Grove, Aberdeen. 26.

DYER, Seaman, HARRY, 3945B. Royal Naval Reserve. Killed by mine explosion off Irish Coast 25th January 1917.
Age 32. Son of William and Sarah Dyer, of Brixham, Devon; husband of Mina Dyer, of 61, Waterloo Rd., Hakin, Milford Haven, Pembrokeshire. 23.

ELLIOTT, Engineer Sub-Lieutenant, GEORGE LITTLETON. Royal Naval Reserve. Killed by mine explosion off Irish Coast 25th January 1917. 23.

EVERSFIELD, Trimmer, STEPHEN, 781584. Mercantile Marine Reserve. Killed by mine explosion off Irish Coast 25th January 1917.
Age 27. Son of Charles Thomas and Ellen Eversfield, of 29, Edward St., Canning Town, London. 25.

EWING, Petty Officer, ROBERT THOMPSON, 231949. Royal Navy. Killed by mine explosion off Irish Coast 25th January 1917.
Age 29. (RFR/DEV/B/4540) Son of Annie Ewing, of Liverpool, and the late David Ewing; husband of Mary Elizabeth Ewing, of 5, St. George St., Everton, Liverpool. 20.

FARLEY, Seaman, JOSEPH, 3747C. Royal Naval Reserve. Killed by mine explosion off Irish Coast 25th January 1917.
Age 32. Son of Jeremiah and Mary Farley, of Scilly, Kinsale, Co. Cork. 23.

FENWICK, Assistant Cook, JOHN, 830647. Mercantile Marine Reserve. Killed by mine explosion off Irish Coast 25th January 1917. 26.

FITZGERALD, Seaman, WALTER, 2465C. Royal Naval Reserve. Killed by mine explosion off Irish Coast 25th January 1917.
Age 36. Son of Catherine Fitzgerald, of Ballymacaw, Dunmore East, Co. Waterford, and the late John Fitzgerald. 23.

FLETCHER, Fireman, JAMES, 873086. Mercantile Marine Reserve. Killed by mine explosion off Irish Coast 25th January 1917. 25.

GARDINER, Fireman, EDWARD, 908142. Mercantile Marine Reserve. Killed by mine explosion off Irish Coast 25th January 1917.
Age 26. Son of Thomas and Alice Gardiner; husband of Catherine Ann Gardiner, of 63, Portland St., Liverpool. 25.

GASSER, Petty Officer Ist Class, JOSEPH HENRY, 120067. Royal Navy. Killed by mine explosion off Irish Coast 25th January 1917. (RFR/DEV/A/1741) 20.

GAULE, Seaman, JAMES, 4972A. Royal Naval Reserve. Killed by mine explosion off Irish Coast 25th January 1917.
Age 27. Son of Kate Gaule, of Youghal, Co. Cork, and the late Mr. Gaule. 23.

GAVIN, Fireman, PETER. Mercantile Marine Reserve. Killed by mine explosion off Irish Coast 25th January 1917.
Age 36. Son of James Gavin, of Castlebar, Co. Mayo; husband of Catherine Gavin, of 13, Iden St., Boundary Place, Liverpool. 25.

GODFREY, Cooper, ALFRED ERNEST. Mercantile Marine Reserve. Killed by mine explosion off Irish Coast 25th January 1917.
Age 28. Son of the late William and Alice Godfrey; brother of Edith Godfrey, of 269, Borough Rd., Birkenhead. 25.

GODFREY, Chief Carpenter, ROBERT ROGER, 594655. Mercantile Marine Reserve. Killed by mine explosion off Irish Coast 25th January 1917. Age 31. Son of Mrs. E. Godfrey, of 4, James St., Seacombe, Cheshire. Born at Wallasey. 25.

GREEN, Greaser, ARTHUR EDWARD. Mercantile Marine Reserve. Killed by mine explosion off Irish Coast 25th January 1917.
Age 38. Son of Edward and Elizabeth Green, of Pythian St., Liverpool. 25.

GREEN, Greaser, NORMAN WILLIAM. Mercantile Marine Reserve. Killed by mine explosion off Irish Coast 25th January 1917.
Age 23. Son of George William and Emily Elizabeth green, of 54, Cundy St., Custom House, London. 25.

GRIFFITHS, Boy, DENIS STEPHEN, J/47837. Royal Navy. Killed by mine explosion off Irish Coast 25th January 1917.
Age 17. Sig. Son of W. H. and F. M. Griffiths, of 21, Old Park H/117 St. Michael's, Bristol. 21.

GRIFFITHS, Leading Seaman, ROBERT ELLIS, 2771A. Royal Naval Reserve. Killed by mine explosion off Irish Coast 25th January 1917.
Age 26. Son of the late Capt. Griffith Griffiths and Dorothy Griffiths, of 15, Gondover Avenue, Aintree, Liverpool. With the Naval Brigade at the fall of Antwerp. Native of Barmouth. 23.

GROVES, Trimmer, FREDERICK THOMAS, 778678. Mercantile Marine Reserve. Killed by mine explosion off Irish Coast 25th January 1917.25.

HAGEN, Seaman, JOHN, 4276A. Royal Marine Reserve. Killed by mine explosion off Irish Coast 25th January 1917. 23.

HAINES, Assistant Steward, WILLIAM COULSTON. Mercantile Marine Reserve. Killed by mine explosion off Irish Coast 25th January 1917.
Age 21. Son of Sarah Ada Hyde (formerly Haines), of Wheeler's Farm, Swallowfield, Reading, Berks, and the late William Haines. Native of Thornton Heath, Surrey. 26.

HALSALL, Trimmer, THOMAS, 852812. Mercantile Marine Reserve. Killed by mine off Irish Coast 25th January 1917.
Age 19. Son of Thomas and Susan Halsall, of Bootle, Liverpool. 25.

HEANEY, Seaman, DANIEL, 4995A. Royal Naval Reserve. Killed by mine explosion off Irish Coast 25th January 1917.
Age 26. Son of Michael and Rosanna Heaney, of 36, Probys Row, Arklow, Co. Wicklow. 23.

HEDGE, Private, JOHN ALFRED, PLY/15351. Royal Marine Light Infantry. Killed by mine explosion off Irish Coast 25th January 1917. 23.

HENNESSEY, Fireman, JAMES ALBRER, 778461. Mercantile Marine Reserve. Killed by mine explosion off Irish Coast 25th January 1917. 25.

HILL, Seaman, WILLIAM JAMES, 2348D. Royal Naval Reserve. Killed by mine explosion off Irish Coast 25th January 1917. Son of George and H. Hill, of London; husband of Harriet Hill, of 47, Scyborfach St., Swansea. 23.

HILTON, Greaser, ALLEN PERCY, 884190. Mercantile Marine Reserve. Killed by mine explosion off Irish Coast 25th January 1917
Age 35. Son of Jane and Christopher Hilton; husband of Elizabeth Mary Hilton, of 17, Imperial Avenue, Freemantle, Southampton. 25.

HOBBS, Shipwright 2nd Class, WILLIAM GEORGE, M/21471. Royal Navy. Killed by mine explosion off Irish Coast 25th January 1917.
Age 21. Son of George and Isabella Hobbs, of 84, Gwyther St., Pembroke Dock. 22.

HOLBROOK, Steward, HENRY STEPHEN, 538989. Mercantile Marine Reserve. Killed by mine explosion off Irish Coast 25th January 1917.
Age 50. Native of Portsmouth. Son of the late George and Mary A. Holbrook, of Portsmouth and London; husband of Mary S. Holbrook, of 49, Cameron St., Kensington, Liverpool. 26.

HOSIER, Scullion, ARTHUR, 851884. Mercantile Marine Reserve. Killed by mine explosion off Irish Coast 25th January 1917.
Age 21. Son of Mr. W. Hosier, of 3, Dakin St., Limehouse, London. 26.

HOYLE, Stoker, WILLIAM CLEVERTON, 3445S. Royal Marine Reserve. Killed by mine explosion off Irish Coast 25th January 1917.
Age 36. Brother of Mrs. Mary Jane Catherine McKeer, of 39, Exeter St., Plymouth. Native of Plymouth. 24.

HUGHES, Seaman, ALFRED GEORGE, 3667A. Royal Marine Reserve. Killed by mine explosion off Irish Coast 25th January 1917. 23.

HUGHES, Steward, WILLIAM GRIFFITH EDWIN, 676630. Mercantile Marine Reserve. Killed by mine explosion off Irish Coast 25th January 1917.
Age 41. Charge son of Edwin and Margaret Hughes, of Llanfair, Harlech, Merionethshire. 26.

HURST, Engineer Commander, CHARLES EDWIN. Royal Naval Reserve. Killed by mine explosion off Irish Coast 25th January 1917.
Age 43. Husband of Emily Hurst, of "Penlee," Litherland Park, Litherland, Liverpool. 23.

ILES, Chief Cook, WILLIAM HENRY, 736333. Mercantile Marine Reserve. Killed by mine explosion off Irish Coast 25th January 1917.
Age 45. Son of Henry and Sarah Iles, of Liverpool; husband of Jessie Iles. 26.

INGHAM, Seaman, ROBERT EDWARD, 2105A. Royal Marine Reserve. Killed by mine explosion off Irish Coast 25th January 1917. 23.

JACKSON, Trimmer, LAURENCE, 867053. Mercantile Marine Reserve. Killed by mine explosion off Irish Coast 25th January 1917. 25.

JAGO, Chief Petty Officer, WILLIAM HARRY, 160954. Royal Navy. Killed by mine off Irish Coast 25th January 1917. 20.

JAMES, Lieutenant, DAVID THOMAS EMYR. Royal Naval Reserve. Killed by mine explosion off Irish Coast 25th January 1917.
Age 31. Son of Capt. David and Annie James, of St. Dogmaels, Pembrokeshire; husband of Annie James, of 12, Earlsfield Rd., Sefton Park., Liverpool. 23.

JAMES, Assistant Steward, HARRY, 457410. Mercantile Marine Reserve. Killed by mine explosion off Irish Coast 25th January 1917. 26.

JAMES, Seaman, JOHN, 3721C. Royal Marine Reserve. Killed by mine explosion off Irish Coast 25th January 1917.
Age 41. Husband of Annie James, of 7, William St., Cardigan. 23.

JAMIESON, Trimmer, ALEX, 697537. Mercantile Marine Reserve. Killed by mine explosion off Irish Coast 25th January 1917. 25.

JAMIESON, Engineer Lieutenant, THOMAS. Royal Naval Reserve. Killed by mine explosion off Irish Coast 25th January 1917. 23.

JAMIESON, Petty Officer, WILLIAM JOHN GLENDORE, 234416. Royal Navy. Killed by mine explosion off Irish Coast 25th January 1917. 20.

JARVIS, Assistant Steward, GEORGE EDWARD, 637485. Mercantile Marine Reserve. Killed by mine explosion off Irish Coast 25th January 1917.
> Age 23. Son of Jane Jarvis; brother of Mrs. R. Raymond, of 4, Approach Rd., Victoria Park, London. 26.

JONES, Steward, HUGH, 619939. Mercantile Marine Reserve. Killed by mine explosion off Irish Coast 25th January 1917. 26.

JONES, Fireman, JAMES, 597150. Mercantile Marine Reserve. Killed by mine explosion off Irish Coast 25th January 1917. 25.

JONES, Steward, JOHN, 726753. Mercantile Marine Reserve. Killed by mine explosion off Irish Coast 25th January 1917.
> Age 29. Son of Mrs. Rose Jones, of 10, Fielding St., Kensington, Liverpool. 26.

KEELY, Sergeant, BERNARD, PLY/4488. (RMR/A/1039) Royal Marine Light Infantry. Killed by mine explosion off Irish Coast 25th January 1917.
> Age 42. Son of Stephen and Hannah Keely, of Plymouth; husband of Maud M.E.Keely, of 31, Pasley St., Stoke, Devenport. 23.

KELLY, Fireman, THOMAS. Mercantile Marine Reserve. Killed by mine explosion off Irish Coast 25th January 1917. Husband of Elizabeth Kelly, of 51, Gun St., Spitalfields, London. 26.

KEWLEY, Seaman, JOSEPH, 4726B. Royal Naval Reserve. Killed by mine explosion off Irish Coast 25th January 1917.
> Age 32. Son of E. and E. M. Kewley, of 3, Shaws Brow, Douglas, Isle of Man. 23.

KIRKHAM, Chief Butcher, WILLIAM, 643228. Mercantile Marine Reserve. Killed by mine explosion off Irish Coast 25th January 1917.
> Age 45. Son of John and Margaret Kirkham, of Toxteth Park, Liverpool. 26.

LACEY, Assistant Cook, JOSEPH. Mercantile Marine Reserve. Killed by mine explosion off Irish Coast 25th January 1917.
> Age 25. Son of Nicholas and Margaret Lacey; husband of Pauline Lacey, of 42, Elstow St., Kirkdale, Liverpool. 26.

LANGTON, Greaser, FRANK, 678257. Mercantile Marine Reserve. Killed by mine explosion off Irish Coast 25th January 1917. Ldg. 26.

LARMOUR, Engineer Lieutenant, EDWARD ARCHIBALD RICE. Royal Naval Reserve. Killed by mine explosion off Irish Coast 25th January 1917.
> Age 36. Son of Annabella Steele (formerly Larmour), of Belfast, and the late Edward Larmour; husband of Johanna Margrietha Larmour, of 1, Stretton Avenue, Wallasey, Cheshire. 23.

LAVERTY, Leading Seaman, WILLIAM AICKEN, 218192. Royal Navy. Killed by mine explosion off the Irish Coast 25th January 1917.
> Age 30. Son of James and Jane Laverty, of 13, Ravenscroft St., Connswater, Belfast. 20.

LAWRENCE, Able Seaman, ERNEST WILLIAM, 211909. (RFR/DEV/B/2434). Royal Navy. Killed by mine explosion off Irish Coast 25th January 1917.
> Age 35. Son of William and Mary Grace Lawrence, of Week St. Mary, Holsworthy, Cornwall. Husband of the late Mrs. Lawrence. 21.

LAWRIE, Fireman, J.H.M.S. Mercantile Marine Reserve. Killed by mine explosion off Irish Coast 25th January 1917. 26.

LEWIS, Chief Engine Room Artificer, ROBERT PRICE, 1461EA. Royal Naval Reserve. Killed by mine explosion off Irish Coast 25th January 1917.
> Age 28. Son of the late Hugh and Hannah Lewis, of Widnes. 24.

LLOYD, Shipwright, WALTER FREDERICK LLEWELLYN, 707093. Mercantile Marine Reserve. Killed by mine explosion off Irish Coast 25th January 1917.
> Age 23. Son of Margaret Lloyd of 85, Lambeth Rd., Kirkdale, Liverpool, and the late John Lloyd. 25.

LODDEY, Petty Officer, SIDNEY WILLIAM, 203282. Royal Navy. Killed by mine explosion off Irish Coast 25th January 1917.
> Age 34. (RFR/DEV/B/4800). Son of the late William and Kate Loddey, of Torquay; husband of Mabel Jane Dewdney (formerly Loddey), of 22, Kenwyn Rd., Ellacombe, Torquay. 20.

LUCAS, Trimmer, HAROLD ARTHUR. Mercantile Marine Reserve. Killed by mine explosion off Irish Coast 25th January 1917.
> Age 20. Son of William Charles Lucas, of 87, Fowler's Walk, Ealing, London. 26.

LUSCOMBE, Petty Officer, ANDREW, 214377. Royal Navy. Killed by mine explosion off Irish Coast 25th January 1917.
> Age 35. Son of George and Emma Luscombe, of South Milton, Kingsbridge, Devon. 20.

MADDOCKS, Greaser, LEONARD ERNEST, 881861. Mercantile Marine Reserve. Killed by mine explosion off Irish Coast 25th January 1917. 26.

MAGNER, Shipwright, JOHN, 562436. Mercantile Marine Reserve. Killed by mine explosion off Irish Coast 25th January 1917. Age 29. Son of John Thomas and Jane Magner, of Birkenhead; husband of Margaret Magner, of 81, Elmswood Rd., Birkenhead. 25.

MAHONEY, Seaman, PATRICK, 2531C. Royal Naval Reserve. Killed in the sinking of the vessel off Irish Coast 25th January 1917.
Age 33. Son of Michael and Catherine Mahoney, of Kinsale; husband of Hannah Mahoney, of 7, Ferry View Terrace, World's End, Kinsale, Co. Cork. 23.

MARSH, Private, ALFRED GEORGE THOMAS, PLY/17972. Royal Marine Light Infantry. Killed by mine explosion off Irish Coast 25th January 1917.
Age 19. Son of Alfred and Ellen Marsh, of 34, Boston Rd., Horfield, Bristol. 23.

MARSHALL, Signalman, HENRY PERCY, Mersey/Z/1637. Royal Naval Volunteer Reserve. Killed by mine explosion off Irish Coast 25th January 1917.
Age 24. Son of William Marshall, of 22, Sedgley Rd., Winton, Bournemouth; husband of Martha H. Watkins (formerly Marshall), of Portswood Rd., Southampton. 25.

MASHEDER, Scullion, WILLIAM. Mercantile Marine Reserve. Killed by mine explosion off Irish Coast 25th January 1917. 26.

MASON, Signalman, ALFRED VERNON, Wales/Z/2496. Royal Naval Volunteer Reserve. Killed by mine explosion off Irish Coast 25th January 1917.
Age 25. Son of Charles Ephraim and Jane Mason, of 29, Lorne St., Stourport, Worcs. 25.

MATTHEWS, Greaser, PAT. Mercantile Marine Reserve. Killed by mine explosion off Irish Coast 25th January 1917. Son of Mary Matthews, of Monasterboice, Drogheda, Co. Louth. 26.

McADAM, Fireman, JAMES. Mercantile Marine Reserve. Killed by mine explosion off Irish Coast 25th January 1917. 26.

McDONALD, Trimmer, ROBERT. Mercantile Marine Reserve. Killed by mine explosion off Irish Coast 25th January 1917.
Age 18. Son of Robert and Minnie McDonald, of 48, Maplin Rd., Custom House, London. 26.

McEVOY, Seaman, JOHN, 3167A. Royal Naval Reserve. Killed by mine explosion off Irish Coast 25th January 1917.
Age 28. Son of the late William and Caroline McEvoy; brother of Mrs. Edith Bell, of 10, Walter St., Bootle, Liverpool. 23.

McGARRY, Fireman, THOMAS, 750721. Mercantile Marine Reserve. Killed by mine explosion off Irish Coast 25th January 1917. 26.

McGREGOR, Trimmer, LESLIE, 851563. Mercantile Marine Reserve. Killed by mine explosion off Irish Coast 25th January 1917. 26.

McKEAN, Leading Seaman, JAMES, 209507. (RFR/DEV/B/5698). Royal Navy. Killed by mine explosion off Irish Coast 25th January 1917.
Age 32. Son of James and Mary Ann McKean, of 24, Canning St., Belfast. 20.

McKIBBIN, Seaman, JOHN EDWARD, 4803B. Royal Naval Reserve. Killed by mine explosion off Irish Coast 25th January 1917.
Age 29. Native of Douglas, Isle of Man. Son of Maria A. McKibbin, of 16, Albemarle Rd., Seacombe, Cheshire, and the late Thomas McKibbin. 23.

McQUADE, Stoker Ist Class, ALEXANDER, 277718. Royal Navy. Killed by mine explosion off Irish Coast 25th January 1917.
Age 50. Son of William and Martha McQuade; husband of Annie Jane McQuade, of 27, Wimbledon St. Belfast. 22.

McVICAR, Engineer Sub-Lieutenant, JOHN. Royal Navy. Killed by mine explosion off Irish Coast 25th January 1917.
Age 27. Son of the late Neil and Isabella McVicar, of Glasgow. 23.

MEEK, Fireman, WILLIAM, 347614. Mercantile Marine Reserve. Killed by mine explosion off Irish Coast 25th January 1917.
Age 38. Native of Greenock. Husband of Davina Meek, of 2, Ingleston St., Greenock. 26.

METCALF, Carpenter's Mate, THOMAS, 510882. Mercantile Marine Reserve. Killed by mine explosion off Irish Coast 25th January 1917. 25.

MIDGLEY, Engineer Sub-Lieutenant, ERNEST EDWARD. Royal Naval Reserve. Killed by mine explosion off Irish Coast 25th January 1917.
Age 28. Son of Elizabeth Midgley, of 16, Buxton Rd., Rock Ferry, Birkenhead, and the late John Charles Midgley. 23.

MILTON, Fireman, JAMES THOMAS, 841321. Mercantile Marine Reserve. Killed by mine explosion off Irish Coast 25th January 1917. 26.

MOLONEY, Seaman, MARTIN, 5237B. Royal Naval Reserve. Killed by mine explosion off Irish Coast 25th January 1917.
    Age 40. Son of Marcin and Ellen Moloney (nee Brown); husband of Bridget Moloney, of Quilty West, Miltown Malbay, Co. Clare. 23.

MOORE, Signalman, JAMES, Bristol/Z/1357. Royal Naval Volunteer Reserve. Killed by mine explosion off Irish Coast 25th January 1917. Son of W.H. and E.E. Moore, of 54, Friezewood Rd., Ashton Gate, Bristol. 25.

MORGAN, Ship's Cook, JOSEPH, 784459. Mercantile Marine Reserve. Killed by mine explosion off Irish Coast 25th January 1917.
    Age 35. Son of the late John and Susannah Morgan, of Liverpool; husband of Ellen Elizabeth Morgan, of 23, Netley St., Kirkdale, Liverpool. 26.

MORRIS, Steward, ALFRED, 675603. Mercantile Marine Reserve. Killed by mine explosion off Irish Coast 25th January 1917.
    Age 22. Son of John and Margaret Morris, of 78, Bedford Rd., Bootle, Liverpool. 26.

MULLANE, Leading Seaman, TIMOTHY, 181569. (RFR/DEV/B/21163). Royal Navy. Killed by mine explosion off Irish Coast 25th January 1917.
    Age 39. Son of John Mullane, of Shangarry, Co Cork; husband of Julia Mullane, of 22, Ethel Rd., Custom House, London. 20.

NEWBERY, Assistant Paymaster, BERNARD CHARLES CROUCHER. Royal Naval Reserve. Killed by mine explosion off Irish Coast 25th January 1917.
    Age 25. Son of Alfred and Winifred Newbery, of 37, Blessington Rd., Lee, London. 23.

NEWMAN, Leading Seaman, GEORGE HENRY, 227726. Royal Navy. Killed in the sinking of the vessel off Irish Coast 25th January 1917.
    Age 31. Son of the late Henry William and Hannah Newman. Native of Dartmouth. 20.

NEWMAN, Seaman, MICHAEL, 2143C. Royal Naval Reserve. Killed by mine explosion off Irish Coast 25th January 1917.
    Age 38. Husband of Annie Newman, of Higher St., Kinsale, Co. Cork. 23.

O'BRIEN, Seaman, JOHN, 2438A. Royal Naval Reserve. Killed by mine explosion off Irish Coast 25th January 1917.
    Age 32. Son of John and Ellen O'Brien, of Youghal, Co. Cork; husband of the late Kate O'Brien. 23.

O'CONNELL, Seaman, MICHAEL, 5170B. Royal Naval Reserve. Killed by mine explosion off Irish Coast 25th January 1917. 23.

O'NEILL, Fireman, MICHAEL. Mercantile Marine Reserve. Killed by mine explosion off Irish Coast 25th January 1917.
    Age 30. Son of Ann O'Neill, of 6, Haddon St., Everton. Liverpool. 26.

O'REILLY, Seaman, THOMAS, 3586A. Royal Naval Reserve. Killed by mine explosion off Irish Coast 25th January 1917.
    Age 29. Son of Mrs. O'Reilly, of 15, Bowles Place, Clare St., Limerick. 23.

O'SULLIVAN, Seaman, THOMAS, 2878B. Royal Naval Reserve. Killed in mine explosion off Irish Coast 25th January 1917.
    Age 32. Son of John O'Sullivan, of 27, Corporation Buildings, Cork; husband of Ellen O'Sullivan, of 16, Dalton's Avenue, Cork. 24.

OLDREY, Fireman, EGBERT HENRY, 861905. Mercantile Marine Reserve. Killed by mine explosion off Irish Coast 25th January 1917.
    Age 52. Son of William John and Eliza Ann Oldrey, of Modbury, Devon. 26.

OLLOSSON, Steward, CHARLES, 681653. Mercantile Marine Reserve. Killed by mine explosion off Irish Coast 25th January 1917. Age 35. Son of Samuel and Mary Ollosson. 26.

ONEY, Greaser, ROSCOE, 844380. Mercantile Marine Reserve. Killed by mine explosion off Irish Coast 25th January 1917. 26.

PALETHORPE, Assistant Baker, FREDERICK, 691933. Mercantile Marine Reserve. Killed by mine explosion off Irish Coast 25th January 1917.
    Age 22. Son of George and Elizabeth Palethorpe, of 4, Antonio St., Bootle, Liverpool. 26.

PARK, Steward, ERNEST GEORGE, 784457. Mercantile Marine Reserve. Killed by mine explosion off Irish Coast 25th January 1917.
    Age 26. Son of Nancy Park, of 12, Ridley Rd., Sheil Rd., Kensington, London. 26.

PARSONS, Mess Room Steward, CHARLES, 591589. Mercantile Marine Reserve. Killed by mine explosion off Irish Coast 25th January 1917. 26.

PARTINGTON, Steward, WILLIAM KIRKHAM TATTON, 579494. Mercantile Marine Reserve. Killed by Mine explosion off Irish Coast 25th January 1917.
    Age 24, Son of William K.T. and Elizabeth Jane Partington, of 14, Victoria Rd., Tue Brook, Liverpool. 26.

PEARSON, Writer, GEORGE, 579371. Mercantile Marine Reserve. Killed by mine explosion off Irish Coast 25th January 1917. 26.

PERRETT, Assistant Cook, J.J. Mercantile Marine Reserve. Killed by mine explosion off Irish Coast 25th January 1917. 26.

PIKE, Chief Petty Officer (pensioner), THOMAS, 149384. Royal Navy. Killed by mine explosion off Irish Coast 25th January 1917.
Age 43. Long Service and Good Conduct Medal. Husband of Agatha Bertha Pike, of 4, Yeoman Terrace, Kingsteignton, Newton Abbot. Served in the South African War. 20.

PIPER, Trimmer, WILLIAM HENRY, 808844. Mercantile Marine Reserve. Killed by mine explosion off Irish Coast 25th January 1917.
Age 24. Son of William Henry and Isabella Piper, of 1, Chapman Rd., Plaistow, London.26.

POUNCEY, Fireman, G.W. Mercantile Marine Reserve. Killed by mine explosion off Irish Coast 25th January 1917. 26.

PROCTOR, Trimmer, ROBERT, 863007. Mercantile Marine Reserve. Killed by mine explosion off Irish Coast 25th January 1917. 26.

QUINLAN, Seaman, THOMAS, 2466C. Royal Naval Reserve. Killed by mine explosion off Irish Coast 25th January 1917.
Age 34. Son of Nicholas and Anastatia Quinlan, of Ballymacaw, Dunmore East, Co. Waterford. 24.

RAFTER, Steward, DANIEL, 623145. Mercantile Marine Reserve. Killed by mine explosion off Irish Coast 25th January 1917.
Age 28. Son of Richard Rafter, of 43, Eastlake St., Everton, Liverpool. 26.

RANDALL, Signalman, THOMAS CHARLES, Bristol Z/1711. Royal Naval Volunteer Reserve. Killed by mine explosion off Irish Coast 25th January 1917.
Age 18. Son of Thomas C. S. and Sarah Randall, of 7, Paragon, Bath. 25.

RANDELL, Seaman, ROBERT, 3601B. Royal Naval Reserve. Killed by mine explosion off Irish Coast 25th January 1917.
Age 34. Son of Mr. and Mrs. A. Randell, of 128, Essex St., Norwich. 24.

RATTIGAN, Fireman, JAMES, 908155. Mercantile Marine Reserve. Killed by mine explosion off Irish Coast 25th January 1917.
Age 21. Son of Patrick and Winifred Rattigan; husband of Mary Rattigan, of 4, St. George's Terrace, Comus St., Liverpool. 26.

REVILLE, Seaman, PATRICK, 2410B. Royal Naval Reserve. Killed by mine explosion off Irish Coast 25th January 1917. 24.

RICH, Steward, CHARLES, 770096. Mercantile Marine Reserve. Killed by mine explosion off Irish Coast 25th January 1917. 26.

RICHARDS, Armourer's Mate, JOHN CHARLES, M/3867. Royal Navy. Killed by mine explosion off Irish Coast 25th January 1917.
Age 28. Native of Ugbourough, Ivybridge. Son of John and Annie Richards, of Blackadon, Ivybridge, Devon. 22.

RILEY, Fireman, THOMAS, 778388. Mercantile Marine Reserve. Killed by mine explosion off Irish Coast 25th January 1917. 26.

ROBERTS, Petty Officer, JAMES DAVID REES, 147492. Royal Navy. Killed by mine explosion off Irish Coast 25th January 1917.
Age 43. (RFR/DEV/A/3584) Long Service and Good Conduct Medal. Husband of Mary Roberts, of 41, Shakespeare Avenue, Milford Haven, Pembrokeshire. Awarded China Medal, 1900. 20.

ROBERTS, Fireman, WILLIAM JOHN. Mercantile Marine Reserve. Killed by mine explosion off Irish Coast 25th January 1917.
Age 30. Son of William and Ellen Roberts, of 40, Ben Johnson Street, Liverpool. 26.

ROCK, Surgeon, FRANK ERNEST. Royal Navy. Killed by mine explosion off Irish Coast 25th January 1917. M.D. 20.

RUSHBROOK, Trimmer, JOHN, 877631. Mercantile Marine Reserve. Killed by mine explosion off Irish Coast 25th January 1917.
Age 17. Son of Alice Ormond, of 110, Elizabeth St., North Woolwich, London. 26.

RUTLEDGE, Engineer Lieut Commander, GEORGE ROBERT. Royal Naval Reserve. Killed by mine explosion off Irish Coast 25th January 1917.
Son of Charles and Annie Rutledge, of New Zealand; husband of Alice E. Rutledge, of New Zealand. 23.

SAXBY-THOMAS, Lieut-Commander, DOUGLAS ROSCOE. Royal Navy. Killed by mine explosion off Irish Coast 25th January 1917. 20.

SCOTT, Boy, ROBERT, J/48888. Royal Navy. Killed by mine explosion off Irish Coast 25th January 1917.
Age 17. Sig. Son of the late John and Jessie Scott, of 11, Castlegreen Terrace, Dumbarton. 21.

SEWELL, Engineer Lieutenant, HUBERT. Royal Naval Reserve. Killed by mine explosion off Irish Coast 25th January 1917.
Age 33. Son of Tom Wilson Sewell and Lavinia Sewell, of Liverpool. 23.

SHERWOOD, Greaser, WILLIAM HENRY THOMAS, 862587. Mercantile Marine Reserve. Killed by mine explosion off Irish Coast 25th January 1917. 26.

SINNOTT, Seaman, THOMAS, 2455A. Royal Naval Reserve. Killed by mine explosion off Irish Coast 25th January 1917. Son of John and Mary Sinnott, of Ballyreilly, Co.Wexford. 24.

SMART, Assistant Cook, GEORGE JOSEPH, 735522. Mercantile Marine Reserve. Killed by mine explosion off Irish Coast 25th January 1917.
Age 36. Son of William and Catherine Smart, of Liverpool; husband of Mary Emma Smart, of 4, Villars St., Liverpool. 26.

SMITH, Greaser, ALFRED ERNEST, 817581. Mercantile Marine Reserve. Killed by mine explosion off Irish Coast 25th January 1917.
Age 26. Son of Mr. and Mrs. J. W. Smith, of London. 26.

SMITH, Trimmer, WILLIAM JAMES, 886725. Mercantile Marine Reserve. Killed by mine explosion off Irish Coast 25th January 1917.
Age 38. Husband of Elizabeth Smith, of 6, York Place, Maroon St., Stepney, London. 26.

SOUTHCOTT, Sick Berth Steward, HENRY JAMES, 350685. Royal Navy. Killed by mine explosion off Irish Coast 25th January 1917.
Age 38. Son of the late Mr. and Mrs. Southcott, of St. Thomas, Exeter; Husband of Helena Southcott. 22.

STARK, Able Seaman (Comm. Boatman CG.). ALFRED JOHN, 128000. Royal Navy. Killed by mine explosion off Irish Coast 25th January 1917.
Age 49. Husband of Brenda Elizabeth Stark, of 18, Park St., Mumbles, Swansea. Native of St. Johns, Torpoint, Cornwall. 21.

STEELE, Assistant Cook, ANDREW, 737290. Mercantile Marine Reserve. Killed by mine explosion off Irish Coast 25th January 1917.
Age 23. Son of Andrew Steele, of 29, Ivy Terrace, Londonderry. 26.

STEELE, Steward, ERNEST THOMAS, 695421. Mercantile Marine Reserve. Killed by mine explosion off Irish Coast 25th January 1917. Brother of Miss F. Steele, of 66, Caulsfield St., Liverpool. 26.

STEVENS, Scullion, GEORGE WILLIAM ROWLAND, 877754. Mercantile Marine Reserve. Killed by mine explosion off Irish Coast 25th January 1917. 26.

THOMAS, Seaman, JOHN WILLIAMS, 1480D. Royal Naval Reserve. Killed by mine explosion off Irish Coast 25th January 1917.
Age 49. Awarded Medal for Zeal (Russia). Son of Edward Thomas and Christian Ann Thomas, of St. Ives; husband of Fanny Gyles Thomas, of Bethesda Place, St. Ives, Cornwall. 24.

THOMPSON, Warrant Telegraphist, RICHARD JAMES. Royal Naval Reserve. Killed by mine explosion off Irish Coast 25th January 1917.
Age 29. Son of John Henry and Annie Thompson, of 4, Oldfield Rd., Sale, Cheshire. 23.

TROY, Petty Officer, ROBERT, 127812. Royal Navy. Killed by mine explosion off Irish Coast 25th January 1917. (RFR/DEV/A/2238) 20.

WALLS, Seaman, JAMES, 1625D. Royal Naval Reserve. Killed by mine explosion off Irish Coast 25th January 1917. 24.

WARBURTON, Signalman, HAROLD JOHN, Mersey/Z/1451. Royal Naval Volunteer Reserve. Killed by mine explosion off Irish Coast 25th January 1917. 25.

WARREN, Fireman, CHARLES EDWARD. Mercantile Marine Reserve. Killed by mine explosion off Irish Coast 25th January 1917.
Age 21. Son of Mrs. Mary Ann August, of 19, Varley Rd., Custom House, London. 26.

WATKINS, Fireman, FREDERICK THOMAS, 809440. Mercantile Marine Reserve. Killed by mine explosion off Irish Coast 25th January 1917.
Age 23. Son of the late William Thomas and Jeanette Watkins, of 20, Broomfield St., Poplar, London. 26.

WEBSTER, Petty Officer, EDMUND HAROLD ORLANDO, 123040. Royal Navy. Killed by mine explosion off Irish Coast 25th January 1917.
Age 51. (RFR/DEV/A/1544) Son of Fredrick, James Webster, of Falmouth. 20.

WIGG, Shipwright, ARTHUR CATCHPOLE. Mercantile Marine Reserve. Killed by mine explosion off Irish Coast 25th January 1917. 25.

WILDMAN, Fireman, ARTHUR ANTHONY, 732193/ Mercantile Marine Reserve. Killed by mine explosion off Irish Coast 25th January 1917.
Age 22. Son of Thomas Anthony and Mary Ann Wildman, of Plaistow, London. 26.

WINKER, Trimmer, THOMAS. Mercantile Marine Reserve. Killed by mine explosion off Irish Coast 25th January 1917. 26.

WINTERTON, Able Seaman, ERNEST, 239256. Royal Navy. Killed by mine explosion off Irish Coast 25th January 1917. 21.

WOODHALL, Fireman, ABEL FRANCIS, 784536. Mercantile Marine Reserve. Killed by mine explosion off Irish Coast 25th January 1917.
Age 23. Son of Abel and Mary Ann Woodhall, of Liverpool; husband of Catherine L. Woodhall, of 245, Smith St., Kirkdale, Liverpool. 26.

WOOLLARD, Fireman, FREDERICK JOHN, 2027D. Royal Naval Reserve. Killed by mine explosion off Irish Coast 25th January 1917.
Age 39. Long Service and Good Conduct Medal. Son of Frederick and Ann Woollard, of 12, Watkin St., Swansea; husband of Catherine Woollard, of 44, Brynmelyn St., Swansea. 24.

YOUNG, Steward, HERMAN LILE, 484890. Mercantile Marine Reserve. Killed by mine explosion off Irish Coast 25th January 1917.
Age 28. Son of William and Bessie Young, of Pembroke Dock; husband of Annie Young, of 36, Thomas St., Holyhead. 26.

PORTSMOUTH NAVAL MEMORIAL-HAMPSHIRE

BATHO, Leading Seaman, PERCY JOHN, 219684. Royal Navy. Killed by mine explosion off Irish Coast 25th January 1917.
Age 31. Son of John Batho, of D'Hautrie Garden, St. Saviour's Hill Jersey. 24.

BLACK, Able Seaman, HUGH. Clyde/5/2423. Royal Naval Volunteer Reserve. Killed by mine explosion off Irish Coast 25th January 1917. 28.

CALDER, Seaman, WILLIAM, 2999A. Royal Naval Reserve. Killed by mine explosion off Irish Coast 25th January 1917.
Age 26. Son of David and Wilhelmina Calder, of Main Street, Lybster, Caithness; husband of Grace Calder, of 8, Wilson St., Thurso. 27.

CONNEELY, Seaman, PATRICK, 5040A. Royal Naval Reserve. Killed by mine explosion off Irish Coast 25th January 1917. 27.

HARDING, Leading Seaman, RICHARD ALFRED, 189014. Royal Navy. Killed by mine explosion off Irish coast 25th January 1917.
Age 38. Son of George and Elizabeth Harding, of Portland, Dorset. 24.

HARTILL, Private, HARRY, PO/17537. Royal Marine Light Infantry. Killed by mine explosion off Irish Coast 25th January 1917.
Age 22. Son of Charlotte Hartill, of 7, Wolverhampton Rd., Wednesfield, Wolverhampton, and the late Thomas Hartill. 27.

KENNEDY, Bombardier, EDWARD, RMA/10168. Head Qrs. (Eastney). Royal Marine Artillery. Killed by mine explosion of Irish Coast 25th January 1917. Husband of the late Florence Kennedy (nee Munday). 26.

KNIGHT, Able Seaman, ALEXANDER, Clyde/2/212. Royal Naval Reserve. Killed by mine explosion off Irish Coast 25th January 1917.
Age 19. Son of Alexander and Annie Knight, of 16, Fort St., Broughty Ferry, Forfarshire. 28.

MAIN, Engine Room Artificer, WILLIAM, 1680EA. Royal Naval Reserve. Killed by mine explosion off Irish Coast 25th January 1917.
Age 26. Son of the late John and Ann Liddell Main. Native of Glasgow. 28.

McGHIE, Engine Room Artificer 4th Class, WILLIAM, West Clyde/311782. Royal Naval Volunteer Reserve. Killed by mine explosion off Irish Coast 25th January 1917.
Age 24. Son of Mr. and Mrs. Nathaniel McGhie, of 30, Gilmour St., Oaklands, Glasgow. 28.

McGREGOR, Seaman, THOMAS, 3752B. Royal Naval Reserve. Killed by mine explosion off Irish Coast 25th January 1917.
Age 31. Son of James McGregor, of 44, Kinnard St., Wick; husband of Johan McGregor, of 31, Smith Terrace, Wick. 27.

McLEAN, Seaman, JAMES, 5278B. Royal Naval Reserve. Killed by mine explosion off Irish Coast 25th January 1917. 27.

McLEAN, Able Seaman, JAMES, Clyde/3/2297. Royal Naval Volunteer Reserve. Killed by mine explosion off Irish Coast 25th January 1917.
Age 36. Son of Margaret McLean, of 34, Murray St., Maryhill, Glasgow. 28.

MILNE, Able Seaman, ROBERT, Clyde/212253. Royal Naval Volunteer Reserve. Killed by mine explosion off Irish Coast 25th January 1917.
Age 22. Son of James and Jane Milne, of 62, Elderslie St., Glasgow. 28.

OLIVER, Seaman, JOHN, 2269A. Royal Naval Reserve. Killed by mine explosion off Irish Coast 25th January 1917.
Age 27. Son of Patrick and Mary Oliver, of Rope Walk, Claddagh, Co. Galway. 27.

PYM. Seaman, FRANK, 4655A. Royal Marine Reserve. Killed by mine explosion off Irish Coast 25th January 1917.
Age 25. Son of Francis Pym, of 131, Perry Gardens, Poole. 27.

REEVES, Seaman, HENRY JOHN, 5172B. Royal Naval Reserve. Killed by mine explosion off Irish Coast 25th January 1917.
Age 27. Son of Robert Henry Reeves, of 12, Junction St., Polegate, Sussex. 27.

REID, Able Seaman, ROBERT ANDERSON, Clyde/211969. Royal Naval Volunteer Reserve. Killed by mine explosion off Irish Coast 25th January 1917.
Age 22. Son of Robert and Mary Anderson Reid, of 79, Earlspark Avenue, Newlands, Glasgow. 28.

REYNOLDS, Seaman, LAURENCE, 4554B. Royal Naval Reserve. Killed by mine explosion off Irish Coast 25th January 1917.
Age 33. Son of James and Mary Reynolds, of Mornington, Drogheda; husband of Anna Reynolds, of 17, Marsh Rd., Drogheda. 27.

SANDISON, Seaman, ROBERT GOUDIE, 1446L. Royal Naval Reserve. Killed by mine explosion off Irish Coast 25th January 1917.
Age 22. Son of Mary A. Sandison, of Catfirth, South Nesting, Shetland, and the late Hunter Sandison. 27.

SMITH, Seaman, JOHN, 3738A. Royal Naval Reserve. Killed by mine explosion off Irish Coast 25th January 1917.
Age 25. Son of Andrew and Ann Smith, of Midgate, Cunningsburgh, Shetland. 27.

SUTHERLAND, Seaman, ANDREW THOMAS, 430L. (Shetland Section.) Royal Naval Reserve. Killed by mine explosion off Irish Coast 25th January 1917.
Age 21. Son of Charles and Wilhelmina Barbara Sutherland, of Tourie, Haroldswick, Unst, Shetland. 27.

TAYLOR, Chief Petty Officer, CHARLES ALBERT, 137905. (RFR/PO/A/3195) Royal Navy. Killed by mine explosion off Irish Coast 25th January 1917. 24.

WEBB, Able Seaman, LEONARD CHARLES, Clyde/4/2270. Royal Naval Volunteer Reserve. Killed by mine explosion off Irish Coast 25th January 1917.
Age 25. Only son of Charles Hall Webb and Rose Harriet Webb, of 8, Ashford Clumps, Ashford, Middx. Native of Tulse Hill, London. 28.

WILCOCKS, Petty Officer, ROBERT, 231604. ("Excellent"). Royal Navy. Killed by mine explosion off Irish Coast 25th January 1917.
Age 28. Son of John Waddington Wilcocks, of Islington, London; husband of Harriet Louise Wilcocks, of 55, High St., Blue Town, Sheerness. 24.

WREN, Able Seaman, JOHN LAWSON, Clyde/3/1979. Royal Naval Volunteer Reserve. Killed by mine explosion off Irish Coast 25th January 1917.
Age 22. Son of Abraham Guthrie Wren and Helen Millar Wren, of "Newton Inn," Mearns, Renfrewshire. Native of Glasgow. 28.

TULLYLISH (ALL SAINTS) CHURCH OF IRELAND CHURCHYARD-COUNTY DOWN

STEELE, Lieutenant, THOMAS. Royal Naval Reserve. Drowned at sea 25th January 1917.
Age 26. Son of the late Alexander Steele; husband of Annie Steele, of 88, Hamilton Rd., Bangor, Co. Down. Born at Gilford, Co. Down. South of Church.

WALLASEY (RAKE LANE) CEMETERY-CHESHIRE

MATHIAS, Commander, J. Royal Naval Reserve. 4th December 1916. 9. R.C. 51.